RIGHT THING, RIGHT NOW

RIGHT THING, RIGHT NOW

GOOD VALUES.
GOOD CHARACTER.
GOOD DEEDS.

RYAN HOLIDAY

Profile Books

First published in Great Britain in 2024 by
Profile Books Ltd
29 Cloth Fair
London
EC1A 7JQ

www.profilebooks.com

First published in the United States by Portfolio,
an imprint of Penguin Random House LLC

Copyright © Ryan Holiday, 2024

Book design by Daniel Lagin

1 3 5 7 9 10 8 6 4 2

Printed and bound in Great Britain by
Clays Ltd, Elcograf S.p.A.

The moral right of the author has been asserted.

A CIP catalogue record for this book is available from the British Library.

ISBN 978 1 78816 631 7
eISBN 978 1 78283 757 2

Injustice is a kind of blasphemy. Nature designed rational beings for each other's sake: to help—not harm—one another, as they deserve. To transgress its will, then, is to blaspheme against the oldest of the gods.

—MARCUS AURELIUS

CONTENTS

Part I: THE ME (PERSONAL)

Part II: THE WE (SOCIOPOLITICAL)

Part III: THE ALL (IS ONE)

The Four Virtues

⁓

It was long ago now that Hercules came to the crossroads.

At a quiet intersection in the hills of Greece, in the shade of knobby pine trees, the great hero of Greek myth first met his destiny.

Where exactly it was or when, no one knows. We hear of this moment in the stories of Socrates. We can see it captured in the most beautiful art of the Renaissance. We can feel his budding energy, his strapping muscles, and his anguish in the classic Bach cantata. If John Adams had had his way, Hercules at the crossroads would have been immortalized on the official seal of the newly founded United States.

Because there, before his undying fame, before the twelve labors, before he changed the world, Hercules faced a crisis, one as life-changing and real as any of us have ever faced.

Where was he headed? Where was he trying to go? That's the point of the story. Alone, unknown, unsure, Hercules, like so many, did not know.

Where the road diverged lay a beautiful goddess who offered

him every temptation he could imagine. Adorned in finery, she promised him a life of ease. She swore he'd never taste want or unhappiness or fear or pain. Follow her, she said, and every desire would be fulfilled.

On the other path stood a sterner goddess in a pure white robe. She made a quieter call. She promised no rewards except those that came as a result of hard work. It would be a long journey, she said. There would be sacrifice. There would be scary moments. But it was a journey fit for a god, the way of his ancestors. It would make him the man he was meant to be.

Was this real? Did it really happen?

If it's only a legend, does it matter?

Yes, because this is a story about us.

About our dilemma. About our own crossroads.

For Hercules the choice was between vice and virtue, the easy way and the hard way, the well-trod path and the road less traveled. The same goes for us.

Hesitating only for a second, Hercules chose the one that made all the difference.

He chose virtue.

"Virtue" can seem old-fashioned. In fact, virtue—*arete*—translates to something very simple and very timeless: Excellence. Moral. Physical. Mental.

In the ancient world, virtue was comprised of four key components.

Courage.

Temperance.

Justice.

Wisdom.

The "touchstones of goodness," the philosopher king Marcus Aurelius called them. To millions, they're known as the "cardinal virtues," four near-universal ideals adopted by Christianity and most of Western philosophy, but equally valued in Buddhism, Hinduism, and just about every other philosophy you can imagine. They're called "cardinal," C. S. Lewis pointed out, not because they come down from church authorities, but because they originate from the Latin *cardo,* or hinge.

It's *pivotal* stuff. It's the stuff that the door to the good life hangs on.

They are also our topic for this book, and for this series.

Four books.* Four virtues.

One aim: to help you choose . . .

Courage, bravery, endurance, fortitude, honor, sacrifice . . .

Temperance, self-control, moderation, composure, balance . . .

Justice, fairness, service, fellowship, goodness, kindness . . .

Wisdom, knowledge, education, truth, self-reflection, peace . . .

---

* This is book 3.

These are the key to the good life, a life of honor, of glory, of *excellence* in every sense. Character traits, which John Steinbeck perfectly described as "pleasant and desirable to [their] owner and makes him perform acts of which he can be proud and which he can be pleased." But the *he* must be taken to mean all of humankind. There was no feminine version of the word *virtus* in Rome. Virtue wasn't male or female, it just *was*.

It still is. It doesn't matter if you're a man or a woman. It doesn't matter if you're physically strong or painfully shy, a genius or of average intelligence. Virtue is universal. The imperative remains universal.

The virtues are interrelated and inseparable, yet each is distinct from the others. Doing the right thing almost always takes courage, just as moderation is impossible without the wisdom to know what is worth choosing. What good is courage if not applied to justice? What good is wisdom if it doesn't make us more modest?

North, south, east, west—the four virtues are a kind of compass (there's a reason that the four points on a compass are called the "cardinal directions"). They guide us. They show us where we are and what is true.

Aristotle described virtue as a kind of craft, something to pursue just as one pursues the mastery of any profession or skill. "We become builders by building and we become harpists by playing the harp," he writes. "Similarly, then, we become just by doing just actions, temperate by doing temperate actions, brave by doing brave actions."

Virtue is something we do.

It's something we choose.

Not once, for Hercules's crossroads was not a singular event. It's a daily challenge, one we face not once but constantly, repeatedly. Will we be selfish or selfless? Brave or afraid? Strong or weak? Wise or stupid? Will we cultivate a good habit or a bad one? Courage or cowardice? The bliss of ignorance or the challenge of a new idea?

Stay the same . . . or grow?

The easy way or the right way?

Introduction

~

Justice, that brightest adornment of virtue by which a good
person gains the title of good.

—CICERO

The clearest evidence that justice is the most important of
all the virtues comes from what happens when you remove
it. It's remarkably stark: The presence of injustice instantly
renders any act of virtue—courage, discipline, wisdom—any
skill, any achievement, worthless . . . or worse.

Courage in the pursuit of evil? A brilliant person with no
morals? Self-discipline to the point of perfect selfishness? There's
an argument that if everyone acted with justice all the time, we
wouldn't have so much need for courage. While discretion moderates bravery and pleasure provides us relief from excessive
self-control, the ancients would point out that there is no virtue
to counterbalance justice.

It just is.

It just *is the whole point.*

Of every virtue. Of every action. Of our very lives.

Nothing is right if we're not doing what is right.

It probably says something about our world today, however, that when people hear the word "justice," their first thought is not of decency or duty but of the legal system. They think attorneys. They think politics. We are concerned with what's lawful, we fight for "our rights" a lot more than *what is right.* It might be too on the nose to call this an "indictment" of modern values, but it's hard to see it as anything else.

"Justice means much more than the sort of thing that goes on in law courts," C. S. Lewis would remind listeners in a famous lecture series. "It is the old name for everything we should now call 'fairness'; it includes honesty, give and take, truthfulness, keeping promises, and all that side of life."

Very simple ideas, yet very rare indeed.

We need to understand that justice isn't simply something between a citizen and the state. Forget due process; what are *you* doing? *Stare decisis?* Justice stares us in the face. Do we act with it? Not only in big moments of responsibility but the little ones—how we treat a stranger, how we conduct our business, the seriousness with which we take our obligations, the way we do our job, the impact we have on the world around us.

Of course, we love to debate justice. *What is it? Whom do we owe it to?* Starting at childhood, nothing animates people more than an argument about fairness, about whether someone has been screwed over or not, about whether we should be allowed to do something. We love vexing hypotheticals, we'll endlessly debate the tricky exceptions to the rules, the moral consequences that prove nobody is perfect.

Modern philosophy twists itself into knots over complicated dilemmas like the so-called trolley problem or whether free will exists. Historians debate the right and wrongness of the military and political and business decisions that have shaped our world, in one turn reveling in the ambiguities while in another making sweeping black-and-white judgments about the endlessly gray.

As if these moral choices are clear and easy, or as if they are one-offs instead of ever present. As if we are the ones asking the question, instead of life asking them of us.

Meanwhile, just in the first few hours of the day, each and every person has made dozens of ethical and moral decisions of no small significance, many of which we do not bother to give even one-tenth of the consideration. As we think about what we might do in some unlikely high-stakes situation, there exist at any moment an *infinite* number of opportunities to engage with these ideas in a real way in real life. Naturally, we prefer justice as an abstraction to distract from having to act—however imperfectly—with justice.

Until we stop debating, we can't start *doing*. We keep debating so we don't have to start doing.

JUSTICE AS A WAY OF LIFE

Earlier in this Stoic Virtues series, we defined courage as putting our ass on the line, and self-discipline as getting your ass in line. To continue this metaphor, we may define justice as *holding the line*—or drawing up our "Flat-Ass Rules," to borrow a phrase from the great General James Mattis. That is, the line between good and evil, right and wrong, ethical and unethical, fair and unfair.

What you will do.

What you won't.

What you *must* do.

How you do it.

Whom you do it for.

What you're willing to give for them.

Is there a certain amount of relativity in all this? Does it sometimes involve trade-offs? Sure, sure, but somehow still in practice, across the ages and across cultures, we find a reassuring amount of timelessness and universality—a remarkable amount of agreement about *the right thing*. You will notice that the heroes in this book, for all their differences—of gender and background, of war and peace, the powerful and the powerless, presidents and the impoverished, activists to abolitionists, diplomats to doctors—are remarkably aligned in matters of conscience and honor. Indeed, the tastes of human beings have changed constantly over the centuries, yet a consensus remains:

We admire those who keep their word. We hate liars and cheats. We celebrate those who sacrifice for the common good, abhor those who grow rich or famous at the expense of others.

No one admires selfishness. In the end, we despise evil and greed and indifference.

Psychologists have reason to believe even infants can feel and understand these notions, which is more evidence still that "the hunger and the thirst for righteousness" is there within us from our earliest days.

The "right thing" is complicated . . . but it's also pretty straightforward.

All the philosophical and religious traditions—from Confucius to Christianity, Plato to Hobbes and Kant—revolve around some version of the golden rule. In the first century BC, Hillel, the Jewish elder, was asked by a skeptic if he could summarize the Torah while standing on one foot. In fact, he could do it in ten words. "Love thy neighbor as thyself," Hillel told the man. "All the rest is commentary."

Care about others.

Treat them as you would wish to be treated.

Not just when it's convenient or recognized, but especially when it isn't.

Even when it's not returned. Even when it costs you.

"The words of truth are simple and justice needs no subtle interpretations, for it hath fitness in itself," the playwright Euripides said, "but the words of injustice, being rotten in themselves, require clever treatment." You know justice when you see it—or, on a more visceral level, you *feel* it, especially its absence and its opposite.

A boy named Hyman Rickover came to America in 1906, his family fleeing the Jewish pogroms of Russia. He worked his way through the US Naval Academy, where he was steeped in the classical virtues. Over a long career, which stretched across thirteen presidents—from Woodrow Wilson to Ronald Reagan—Rickover quietly became one of the most powerful men in the world, pioneering the idea of nuclear ships and submarines, ultimately heading programs responsible for billions of dollars of machinery, tens of thousands of soldiers and workers, along with weapons of enormous destructive potential. Across six decades and global wars in which the threat of apocalyptic nuclear conflict was ever present, when even just an accident at a nuclear facility or onboard a ship could have devastating consequences, Rickover came to wield influence over a generation of the best and brightest officers in the world.

Rickover sometimes told these future leaders that a person should act as if the fate of the world rested on their shoulders—paraphrasing Confucius actually—and this was something that was, at times in his career, quite nearly true. But Rickover was also just a regular human being, someone with a temper, someone with colleagues and subordinates, a spouse, a son, parents, neighbors, bills to pay, traffic to navigate. What guided him, what he spoke about repeatedly in speeches and briefings, was the importance of this idea of a sense of right and wrong, a sense of duty and honor that would guide a person through the infinite dilemmas and decisions they would find themselves in. "Life is not meaningless for the man who considers certain actions wrong simply because they are wrong, whether or not they violate the law," he once explained. "This kind of moral code gives a person a focus, a basis on which to conduct himself."

That kind of code is what this book is about. There will be no complicated legalism or clever witticisms. We will not explore the biological or metaphysical roots of right and wrong. While we will consider the profound moral dilemmas of life, the purpose will be to cut through them—as the human beings who lived through them had to do—not bog you down with hopeless abstractions. There will be no grand theory of the law here, nor will there be any offers of heaven or threats of hell. The aim in this book is much simpler, much more practical—following in the tradition of the ancients who saw justice as a habit or a craft, a way of living.

Because that's what justice should be—not a noun but a verb.

Something we do, not something we get.

A form of human excellence.

A statement of purpose.

A series of actions.

In a world of so much uncertainty, in a world where so much is out of our control, where evil does exist and regularly goes unpunished, the commitment to live rightly is a redoubt in the storm, a light in the dark.

This is what we are after, affixing justice as north on our compass, the North Star to our lives, letting it guide and direct us, through good times and bad. As it did for Harry S. Truman and Gandhi alike, Marcus Aurelius and Martin Luther King Jr., Emmeline Pankhurst and Sojourner Truth, Buddha and Jesus Christ.

When Admiral Rickover slammed down the receiver at the end of a phone call, or brought a meeting to a close, he didn't belabor his exacting expectations or give specific instructions on how he wanted something done. Instead he would leave his subordinates with something that was at once much higher level and yet also clarifyingly down to earth:

"Do what is right!"

So we might end this introduction with that same command:

Do what is right.

Do it right now.

For yourself.

For others.

For the world.

And in these pages, we'll discuss how.

PART I
THE ME
(PERSONAL)

The virtue of a person is measured not by his outstanding efforts but by his everyday behavior.

—BLAISE PASCAL

The pursuit of justice does not begin in far-flung places. It begins at home. It begins with you. It begins with the decision about *who you are going to be*. The old-fashioned values of personal integrity, of honesty, of dignity and honor. The basic behaviors in which these ideals manifest themselves: Doing what you say. Doing business the right way. Treating people well. The Stoics said that the chief task in life is to focus on what you control. Injustice and unfairness and outright cruelty may well rule the world, but it is within the power of each of us to be an exception to that rule. To be a person of *rectitude* and *dignity*. Whatever the law, whatever the culture, whatever we could get away with, we can choose to adhere to our own code—a rigorous and just code. Some might feel that all this is restrictive. We find that the opposite is true: Our code frees us, gives us meaning, and, most of all, makes a positive difference. We preach this gospel not with words but with actions—knowing that each action is like a lantern that hollows out the dark, each decision to do the right thing a statement that our peers, children, and future generation can hear.

To Stand Before Kings . . .

~

It was perhaps the most precarious moment in the history of the world. A beloved president lay in state. A war raged on two fronts. In Europe, the killing continued and the death camps kept firing their awful furnaces and gas chambers. In the Pacific, the long campaign to take island after island ground on, bringing closer each day a dreaded invasion that would dwarf the landing at Normandy.

A ghastly nuclear age—still shrouded in secrecy—had just begun. A racial reckoning, hundreds of years delayed, could not be avoided. The storm clouds of a cold war between great, victorious powers loomed on the horizon.

There, as millions of lives hung in the balance, as uncertain, difficult times beckoned, a man was to meet his moment. Who had the gods sent? What had destiny produced for this crucible?

A small-town Missouri farmer. A short man with glasses so thick and concave they made his eyes bulge. A failed clothing store owner who didn't graduate from college. A former senator from one of the most corrupt states in the country, who had entered politics having failed at nearly everything he'd done in his life. A vice presidential pick that the now-deceased Franklin Roosevelt had barely bothered to brief for the job.

The moment met the man: Harry S. Truman.

The shock of it soon gave way to dread, not just to the people of the United States and the armies abroad, but in Truman himself. "I don't know if you fellas ever had a load of hay fall on you," Roosevelt's successor would tell the press, "but when they told me what happened yesterday, I felt like the moon, the stars, and all the planets had fallen on me." And when Truman asked if he could do anything for the former first lady, Roosevelt's grieving widow shook her head somberly and said, "Is there anything we can do for *you*? For you're the one in trouble now."

Yet not all despaired. "Oh, I felt good," one of the most powerful and experienced men in Washington would reflect, "because I *knew* him. I knew what kind of man he was." Indeed, the people who actually knew Truman were not concerned at all, because, as a Missouri railroad foreman who'd met the future president when the boy was supporting his mother on $35 a month said, Truman was "all right from his asshole out in every direction."

And so began what we might call an incredible experiment, in which a seemingly ordinary person was thrust not just into the limelight but into a position of nearly superhuman responsibility. Could an average person succeed at such a monumental task? Could they not only keep their character intact but prove that character actually counted for something in this crazy modern world?

The answer for Harry Truman was yes. Absolutely yes.

But this experiment did not begin in Washington. Nor in 1945. It began many years earlier with the simple study of virtue, and the example of a man we have already studied in this series. "His real name was Marcus Aurelius Antoninus," Truman would later recount, "and he was one of the great ones." We don't know who introduced Truman to Marcus, but we know what Marcus introduced to Truman. "What he wrote in his *Meditations*," Truman explained of the worldview he borrowed from the emperor, was "that the four greatest virtues are moderation, wisdom, justice, and fortitude, and if a man is able to cultivate those, that's all he needs to live a happy and successful life."

It would be with this philosophy, and the teachings of his parents, that Truman built a kind of personal code of conduct. One that he lived by unfailingly, in moments high and low. "If it's not right, do not do it," Truman underlined in his well-worn copy of *Meditations,* "if it is not true, do not say it. . . . First do nothing thoughtlessly or without a purpose. Secondly, see that your acts are directed to a social end."

Truman was punctual. He was honest. He worked hard. He didn't cheat on his wife. He paid his taxes. He disliked attention or ostentatiousness. He was polite. He kept his word. He helped his neighbors. He carried his own weight in the world. "Since childhood at my mother's knee," Truman would recount, "I

4

have believed in honor, ethics, and right living as its own reward."

It was good that he thought of it as its own reward, because for many years, there was not much more in it for him than that.

After high school, Truman tried his hand as a mailroom boy at the *Kansas City Star,* a drugstore cashier, a timekeeper for the Santa Fe Railroad, a bank clerk, and a farmer. He was rejected first from West Point for his poor eyesight and then second— and in fact repeatedly—by the love of his life, Bess Wallace, whose family did not think he was good enough.

So he struggled on, making ends meet—just barely. Waiting for a chance to prove himself.

The first one came exactly twenty-seven years before Truman entered the White House, when he took his first trip out of the country, landing in the city of Brest, France, as a member of the American Expeditionary Forces, the captain of Battery D, an artillery unit. The list of Truman's plausible exemptions from service in World War I is long. He was thirty-three years old, well past the draft age. He'd already done his time in the National Guard. His eyes were terrible. And as a farmer and the sole breadwinner for his sister and mother, no one expected him to enlist. Yet it was unconscionable to him that someone else would serve in his place. Stirred by Woodrow Wilson's call to make the world safe for democracy—to work toward a "social end," as the Stoics had taught him—he signed up and went.

It was here, suddenly, that his strict code of personal conduct was first put up in front of other people.

"You know justice is an awful tyrant," Truman would write in a letter home, reflecting on the discipline he had to exert over his men, meting out strict but fair punishment to transgressors. Yet he was also the same kind of leader who risked a court-martial to give them an extra night of rest as the war raged, and who was, many years later, still frequenting businesses owned by men in Battery D to help keep them afloat.

After the war, Truman started a clothing store, which was successful just long enough to give him hope, to feel like his bad luck was over. It would shortly become another business failure, leaving him with debts he'd feel so honor bound to repay that he was still carrying (and servicing) them fifteen years later, well into his political career.

In fact, it was those very debts that compelled him to enter politics. "I have to eat," were his words when he went hat in hand to an army buddy, Jim Pendergast, the nephew of Kansas City's all-powerful political boss. Tom Pendergast, who controlled all the offices and patronage for the state, was willing to look kindly on his beloved nephew's friend and allowed him to run for Jackson County court judge in 1922.

If one were writing the backstory for a corrupt politician, Truman's real life would be sympathetic to even the most cynical audience. He had been a good man. He had served his country. He had witnessed his own father dabble in local politics as the overseer of roads in Grandview, Missouri, in 1912, a position where corruption wasn't just common, it was accepted—practically part of the political process. And yet Harry's father, despite being broke, resisted the temptation to cheat his neighbors and line his own pockets. The job ground his father down, and two years later he would be dead, leaving the family with nothing but debts—a tradition Harry seemed primed to continue.

There Harry was, bankrupt and desperate for a job, anointed into politics by one of the most corrupt and wealthy bosses in the country, holding in part the position his father had held. This was his chance to make some money! To show his wife that he was somebody special. To make his place in the world.

Instead, he would prove himself, in Pendergast's words, to be the "contrariest goddamn mule in the world." Setting out to build a courthouse for the county, Truman drove thousands of miles on his own dime to scout buildings and architects. When construction began, he drove to the building site every day and supervised, refusing to allow theft or grift or shoddy work. "I was taught that the expenditure of public money is a public trust," he explained, "and I have never changed my opinion on that subject. No one has ever received any public money for which I was responsible unless he gave honest service for it." Contractors from the political machine sent to Truman were shocked when he actually wanted to see bids—and that he didn't seem to favor local business over better, more efficient companies from out of state. *You'll get contracts from me,* he said, *when you give me the lowest bid.* He would later estimate that he could have stolen as much as $1.5 *million* from the county in his time in office.

Instead, he saved them many times that.

"On April 30th, 1929, after Harry had assigned something over $6 million in road contracts," his biographer David Mc-Cullough would write, "a judgment of default for $8,944.78 was brought against him for his old haberdashery debts. His mother, meantime, had been forced to take another mortgage on the farm. Yet when one of his new roads cut 11 acres from her property, he felt he must deny her the usual reimbursement from the county, as a matter of principle, given his position."

"Looks like everybody in Jackson County got rich but me," Truman would write to his wife, Bess. "I'm glad I can sleep well even if it is a hardship on you and Margie for me to be so damn poor." To his daughter, he would admit he was a financial failure, but say with pride that he had tried to leave her "something that (as Mr. Shakespeare says) cannot be stolen—an honorable reputation and a good name."

As it happened, it was this frustrating and dogged fastidiousness that eventually propelled Truman's career past the local level, "kicking him upstairs," so to speak, into Missouri's open Senate seat. Surely it couldn't hurt to have a man in Washington, but mostly Pendergast, who had known never to ask Truman to do anything unethical, wanted somebody more typical—more *amenable*—in the job closer to home.

Of course, that's not how the people in Washington saw it. The colleagues who didn't snub Truman as a hick referred to him as the "Senator from Pendergast," assuming he was bought and purchased. All Truman could do was return to Marcus Aurelius, particularly a passage he'd marked up with the note "*True! True! True!*"

> When men say injurious things about you, approach their poor souls, penetrate within, and see what kind of men they are. You will discover that there is no reason to take trouble that these men have a good opinion of you. However, you must be well disposed towards them, for by nature they are friends.

Truman toiled away in obscurity as a senator, failing to make an impression with the public until 1941 when his Subcommittee on War Mobilization began to investigate wartime contracts. Suddenly, the man's experiences with temptation and municipal corruption came in handy—he knew how the system worked, he knew where the bodies would be buried. And having watched the hypocritical scrutiny to which politicians and the press had subjected New Deal money that was intended to help the desperate poor, Truman was in no mood to "tolerate" the waste those same groups were willing to accept when it came to defense contractors.

What became known as the "Truman Committee" would, according to a *Time* profile in 1943, give "red faces to cabinet members, war agency heads, generals, admirals, big businessmen, little businessmen and labor leaders." It would end up saving American taxpayers roughly $15 billion and send corrupt officials, including two brigadier generals, to jail.

"I'm hoping to make a reputation as a Senator," Truman had written to his wife, "though if I live long enough that'll make the money successes look like cheese. But you will have to put up with a lot if I do it because I won't sell influence and I'm perfectly willing to be cussed if I'm right."*

Today, with our extensive (though insufficient) campaign finance laws and other forms of legal compliance, perhaps this all seems rather minor. The fact that corruption seems obviously wrong and shameful makes it easy to miss just how remarkable and solitary Truman's honest political life was—it is one thing to try to keep your hands clean, it's another to manage to do it in a den of thieves.

Perhaps you don't see why it matters whether a president insists on paying the postage for letters he sends to his sister—

---

* Meanwhile, in the middle of his campaign in 1940, Truman's mother's farm was sold at auction on the courthouse steps.

"Because they were personal. There was nothing official about them." But that's the point. You're either the kind of person who draws ethical lines like that or you're not. You either respect the code or you don't.

Was it this honesty and the goodwill it engendered that had convinced FDR to choose Truman as his running mate? Or did FDR pick him because the man wasn't much of a threat? All we know is that in April 1945, FDR succumbed to a stroke during a break in Warm Springs, Georgia, and suddenly the ordinary man was president.

Though neither the lure of money nor the temptations of notoriety had dented his character to this point, one could be forgiven for assuming that perhaps total power might finally do it. But that didn't affect Truman's self-discipline either. Before he took office, he had been a punctual man. It had been ingrained early, from his school days, where students were expected, according to the rulebook, "to be punctual and regular in attendance; obedient in spirit; orderly in action; diligent in study; gentle and respectful in manner." And now that he was president, even though all would have waited on him without complaint, it remained unthinkable to him to be late. "When he went to lunch," one of his clerks would explain, "if he left word that he'd return at 2:00 p.m., he was back without fail, not at 2:05, not at 1:15, but at 2:00 p.m."

There were four clocks on the Resolute Desk in the Oval

Office, plus two in the room and one on his wrist. Even his walking, which had been trained into him in the army, was on time—always 120 steps per minute. Hotel clerks and reporters could set their own watches to Truman's daily routine. "Oh, he'll be stepping off the elevator at 7:29 a.m.," they'd say whenever he visited New York.

And he would! Without fail!

Not long after assuming office, Truman had what he thought was an ordinary conversation with Harry Hopkins, one of Roosevelt's longest-serving aides and confidants, after sending him on an emergency mission to Russia. "I'm exceedingly obligated to you for what you did," Truman told him, "and I want to thank you for it." Hopkins was stunned, and, leaving the office, said to the press secretary, "You know, I've just had something happen to me that never happened before in my life . . . The President just said, 'Thank you,' to me."

Truman was the kind of man who, when a cabinet member's daughter had an operation while her father was overseas on state business, called the envoy with updates on her condition *from the hospital*; who, after a terse exchange with a college student in California, asked the boy to write to him and asked the dean to keep him informed of the boy's grades; who, in the middle of the Berlin Airlift, would send a note of condolence from the White House when the child of a Battery D veteran died in a car accident; and who, finally, would bring former president Hoover to tears by inviting him back to the White House after twelve years of exile.* But the public's first glimpse of this personal affection and empathy came just six days after his swearing in, when Truman attended the funeral of Tom Pendergast, a persona non grata after a prison sentence and fall from grace. "What kind of man wouldn't go to his friend's funeral because he'd be criticized for it?" Truman asked.

It takes a special kind of person to even have the bandwidth to care about other people during what was arguably the most stressful period of their life and quite possibly one of the most stressful periods for literally everyone alive at that moment. In the span of thirty days, the Soviets were interfering in Poland and entering the war against Japan, while the UN was forming to prevent future world wars and the first shipment of uranium was en route for military use.

"He is a man of immense determination," Winston Churchill would say of Truman shortly after meeting him. "He takes no notice of delicate ground, he just plants his foot down firmly on it." Good thing, because the next several months would bring the economic collapse of Europe, the Berlin Airlift, and the implementation of the Truman Doctrine.

The most consequential of his decisions in that period was, of course, the dropping of the atomic bombs on Hiroshima and

---

*He assigned Hoover a role in delivering food and supplies to Europe, which had actually been Hoover's specialty after World War I and during the Great Flood of 1927.

Nagasaki. The debate over this decision rages now and it raged immediately after, but one overlooked fact is how little debate raged before. Just months prior to the first explosions of the nuclear age, Truman did not even know the bomb existed! It was a military project and primarily a military decision, with one general later describing Truman as a "little boy on a toboggan who never had an opportunity to say yes. All he could say was no." It was more complicated than that, as Truman himself noted on the very day of the first tests, lamenting a world where "machines are ahead of morals by some centuries," and hoping for a future where such a thing would not exist.

But there in the present, he battled an implacable and almost incomprehensibly evil foe. On July 30, 1945, the USS *Indianapolis,* the ship that had just four days prior delivered to Tinian Island the materials to assemble the first nuclear bomb, was sunk by a Japanese submarine. Over a thousand men died, many eaten by sharks as they floated in the ocean.

We know that Truman decided not to say no—believing for the rest of his life that this was the correct call, that as a president elected by millions of mothers and fathers, his duty was to protect American lives over most other considerations. Yet after the devastation wrought on August 6 and 9 the implications of this decision were brought into full, atomic relief. While the incineration of more than two hundred thousand Japanese is a tragedy that will be etched in human history forever, one critical outcome was Truman's sense afterward that such horrible power could not under any circumstances be left in the hands of military officials. Treading firmly on delicate ground, he asserted civilian control over nuclear weapons, where it has remained—thankfully—and they have yet to be used again.

It's almost a cliché of leadership stories now to point out that on his desk in the White House, Truman had a little sign that read "The Buck Stops Here." This was true and it did embody his approach—which was not just to make tough decisions but to take responsibility for them too. Lesser known, however, is a more illustrative sign, one that far more leaders today could stand to follow. "Always do right!" it read, quoting Mark Twain. "This will gratify some people and astonish the rest."

Was the use of nuclear weapons right? It remains debated. No one, on the other hand, questions the Marshall Plan. When Germany surrendered in May 1945, it was hardly the end of Europe's problems. Both the continent and Britain had been ravaged by six years of war. Some forty million people had been displaced. A generation of children were orphaned. Across enormous swaths of an entire continent, people were without jobs or heat or food. If the war had been a humanitarian calamity, killing millions, the suffering set to follow would have been incomprehensible.

Resolved to do something, Truman and his advisors hardened on an economic rescue of an entire hemisphere. He told Congress he'd need $15 or $16 *billion* to give away. When Sam Rayburn, the Speaker of the House, balked, Truman reminded him that that was almost exactly the amount that the Truman Commission had saved the country some years earlier. "Now we're going to need that money," he told him, "and we could save the world with it."

If this plan was all Truman's doing, why isn't it named after him? Political acumen is one reason. Midwestern modesty is another. "General, I want the plan to go down in history with your name on it," Truman would tell General George Marshall, the wildly popular architect of the Allied war effort at home, whom he had known since his days as a soldier in World War I. "And don't give me any argument. I've made up my mind, and, remember, I'm your commander in chief." And so what the historian Arthur Toynbee would call the "signal achievement of our age"—the giving of billions of dollars to ravaged, war-torn nations, and in some cases to former enemies—was topped off with a simple act of humility, the giving of the credit to someone else.

There have been plenty of leaders of great personal integrity who had abysmal records on human rights. The tragic irony of both America's crusade in Europe and the Pacific—fighting against fascism and genocide and for democracy and the rule of law—is just how imperfect its union was at home. Truman had grown up in a former slave state, just a generation removed from slavery, and retained well into adulthood much of the repugnant racial baggage that comes with that kind of upbringing. His grandparents on both sides had owned slaves. His parents remembered the Civil War vividly enough—or incorrectly enough—that Truman's own mother refused to sleep in the Lincoln Bedroom when she visited her son in the White House.

So you have a man who was raised by racists to be a racist, who had casually considered joining the Ku Klux Klan in 1922 like it was any other of the dozen or so social clubs he was a member of, transforming into the man who desegregated the armed forces in 1948 (one of the few things the president could do unilaterally). Then this same man banned discrimination across the federal government, in a stroke opening up thousands of jobs to Americans regardless of race or religion or nationality. It was Truman who held the first integrated political rally in the state of Texas in 1948, and then became the first president to address the NAACP, speaking on the steps of the Lincoln Memorial. But years before that, in Sedalia, Missouri, it was Truman who stared down his own neighbors and kin and challenged them on the topic of race. "I believe in the brotherhood of man," he told them, "not merely the brotherhood of white men but the brotherhood of all men before the law. I believe in the Constitution and the Declaration of Independence. In giving Negroes the rights which are theirs we are only acting in accord with our own ideals of a true democracy."

He could have done more—everyone could have—but what he did do his advisors told him was all but "political suicide." In 1948, he saw what they meant, as many Southern states walked out of the Democratic National Convention in Philadelphia over his civil rights policies. He lost some support, he'd admit, but replied bravely, "You can always get along without the support of people like that."

Why had he ventured into this? Sure, it was because he believed in the Constitution and the Declaration of Independence. In his Lincoln Memorial speech, he presaged Martin Luther King Jr.'s famous dream some sixteen years later by saying "when I say all Americans, I mean *all* Americans." But mostly it was news of a horrible lynching in Monroe, Georgia, of a black World War II veteran, one explicitly encouraged by local politics. It was the sheer cruelty and violence of it that had disabused Truman of any of his childhood illusions. It offended his sense of decency and basic humanity. "My God!" he said when told of the way that a uniformed Sergeant Isaac Woodard Jr. had been pulled off a bus in South Carolina then beaten and deliberately blinded in both eyes by a local police chief. "I had no idea it was as terrible as that," he said. "We've got to do something!"

And he did.

The Presidential Commission on Civil Rights he created shortly thereafter would significantly change the arc of justice in America, beginning the transformation that had not only been too long delayed, but that Truman himself had ignored. "The wonderful, wonderful development in those years," the White House counsel would observe, "was Harry Truman's capacity to grow."

In 1950, he heard that the family of Sergeant John Rice was

having trouble burying their son at *any* of the cemeteries in Sioux City, Iowa. Rice, a war hero in the Pacific, had been killed in action in Korea, shortly before the landing at Inchon. He also happened to be a Native American who went by the name Walking in Blue Sky. Truman, outraged at the injustice, cleared the way for Rice to be buried at Arlington, with full military honors and a plane sent for his family. "The President feels that the national appreciation of patriotic sacrifice should not be limited by race, color or creed," went the official statement.

There was little in Harry Truman that resembled Franklin Roosevelt or Abraham Lincoln. He gave few sweeping speeches; nobody saw him as a great man of history. He was short. He wasn't handsome. He did not exude class or power or social grace. His decisions weren't the product of some cohesive ideology. They were rooted less in some grand vision of the future than in something much simpler and more accessible—something more human too. What our own conscience and self-respect demands we provide to others, in how we treat others.

Truman wasn't perfect and, like all men, was a product of his time—frustratingly clinging to prejudices and conventions longer than he should have. But still, it should inspire us that that the White House butler, Alonzo Fields, a black man who served under four presidents across two decades, reflected that Truman was the only powerful person he met who *took the time to understand him as a person.*

How many politicians are honest? How many are kind? How

many live by a code? How many people put others first? "I have read over and over again that he was an ordinary man," Dean Acheson, Truman's Ivy League–educated, blue-blooded secretary of state, would say. "Whatever that means ... I consider him one of the most extraordinary human beings who ever lived."

Perhaps nothing proves this more than who Truman was *after* office. Deciding not to run for a third term (a precedent blown apart by Roosevelt), Truman was faced with the reality of handing over office to Dwight D. Eisenhower, a man whom he had long admired but watched develop into a rather ungrateful political adversary.*

After a bitter campaign, where both attacked each other personally, the day of the inauguration was a fraught one. Eisenhower had won in an enormous landslide, but he was not feeling particularly magnanimous. He snubbed a gracious invitation from Truman for coffee at the White House, trying to force Truman to pick him up from his hotel. Only reluctantly did Eisenhower agree to call on the sitting president—as precedent dictated—only to wait in the car so as to force Truman to come to him, which Truman did without issue.

There, at the steps of the Capitol, Eisenhower was shocked to

---

*Truman personally destroyed evidence that Eisenhower cheated on his wife during the war, believing it nobody's business, and, according to some accounts, offered not to run for reelection if Eisenhower wanted the presidency.

find that his son, then in the army overseas, was in attendance. "I wonder who is responsible for my son John being ordered to Washington from Korea?" Eisenhower demanded. "I wonder who is trying to embarrass me?" Truman, who had quietly planned this thoughtful surprise on behalf of his now rival, could only reply, "The President of the United States ordered your son to witness the swearing-in of his father to the Presidency. If you think somebody was trying to embarrass you by this order then the President assumes full responsibility." A few days later, Eisenhower would send Truman a letter acknowledging his "thoughtfulness in ordering my son home from Korea . . . and even more especially for not allowing either him or me to know that you had done so." And he then repaid this graciousness by not speaking to Truman for another six years.

Leaving Washington, his car stopping at red lights for the first time in nearly a decade, Truman returned to Independence, Missouri. He'd be asked by reporters what he did on his first day out of office. *I carried our suitcases up to the attic*, he replied, returning painlessly to the life he lived and the person he was before the presidency—which is to say, a regular person. Not long after, he was spotted by the side of the highway, having gotten out to help a farmer herd their pigs off the road.

Truman, like many ex-presidents, was besieged by lucrative opportunities—do-nothing jobs that would have finally made him secure and rich. He turned them all down. "I'd rather die in the poorhouse than do a thing like that," he said. Indeed, the country came to fear that might well happen and had to, no doubt to the man's great embarrassment, create the first presidential pension.

In office, Truman said several times while awarding the Congressional Medal of Honor that he'd rather have such a medal himself than be president of the United States. Yet at eighty-seven years old, Truman preemptively turned down the award from Congress. "I do not consider that I have done anything which should be the reason of any award, Congressional or otherwise," he wrote. "This does not mean I do not appreciate what you and others have done, because I do appreciate the kind things that have been said and the proposal to have the award offered to me."

The Medal of Honor was for heroism in battle, he felt, and rules were not be bent in in his favor. Even for the thing he wanted more than anything.

Such was the man.

Such is the example we must try to follow.

Even if very few people agree with us on it. Even if it's not exactly rewarded.

We must understand: Justice is not this thing we demand of other people, but something we demand of ourselves. It's not a thing we talk about, it's a way of life. Nor must it be always an abstract, cosmic thing. It can be practical, accessible, and personal. Indeed, where else better to start?

Justice can be . . .

. . . the standards we hold ourselves to

. . . the way we treat people

. . . the promises we keep

. . . the integrity we bring to our words

. . . the loyalty and generosity we give to our friends

. . . the opportunities we accept (and turn down)

. . . the things we care about

. . . the difference we make for people.

This won't always be popular. It won't always be appreciated. Truman would leave office as one of the most unpopular presidents in history, as most leaders who make difficult but necessary decisions usually are. But his actions have aged well, as ethics and honor usually do.

We keep doing the right thing and in the end, it keeps us . . .

. . . and indeed, the world too.

Keep Your Word

~

Marcus Atilius Regulus had the Carthaginians on the ropes in 256 BC, but it was not to be. His enemies, boosted by the help of the Spartans, defeated the Romans in a surprise reversal at the Battle of Tunis. Just a few months after lording impossible surrender terms over his opponents, Regulus was now a prisoner of war.

He would languish in Carthage for five years, almost a thousand miles from Rome, away from his family, reduced to slavery, dressed in rags, hopeless and helpless. All seemed lost, until again, after yet another reversal on the battlefield, Carthage wanted peace and sent him back to Rome to negotiate a prisoner swap and an end to the hostilities.

Free of Carthage, the sea wind in his face, Regulus headed home. The war hero back after so many years away. Back from the dead. Back with his family. Far from the clutches of the enemy.

Except Regulus had advice to offer the Roman Senate after he explained Carthage's terms: Reject the offer. Carthage was weak, he said, or they wouldn't have sent me as leverage. Fight on. *The war was winnable.*

Grateful, the Romans followed his advice . . . and Regulus packed his bags. Not to rejoin the army, but *to return to Carthage, as a prisoner.* His friends were stunned. You're safe now, why would you return? "I have sworn to them to return," Regulus explained of the honor system he had been paroled on. "I will not transgress my oaths, not even when they have been given to enemies."

He had given his word. That was it.

But us? We're trying to wiggle out of that thing we just agreed to. Trying to weasel out an exemption so we don't have to keep our promise. Because something better came up. Because something more lucrative came in. Because it became clear just how hard it was going to be. Because we don't think it really says anything about us.

Yeah, it's true, keeping your word can cost you. You'll get stuck doing something you'd rather not. You'll have to pass on the better opportunity that came after you'd already agreed to do something else. By sticking to what you've agreed to, you end up with something worse than market price.

But it's not without cost to break your word either. Nor is your reputation usually the only one at stake. Not only because we all represent other people, but because each time we deceive or break faith, we undermine the public trust—we make it hard for people to trust each other.

But the converse is also true: Each time we keep our word, we make a deposit, we add a strand to the rope that binds the world together.

Toward the end of his life, as his health failed, Harry Truman had to start canceling interviews and appearances. "I'm very sorry I wasn't out there this morning," he told a reporter he'd had to reschedule with. "That's all right, Mr. President. You were ill." "I know," Truman said, his eyes tearing up, "but I like to live up to my obligations."

Is there anyone we admire who *doesn't* try to live up to their obligations? Who doesn't keep their word?

We keep our word to ourselves—that's discipline.

We keep our word to others because it's justice.

When someone says they're going to meet a deadline, that it would cost this or that much, to consider the project approved, that they'd be there—people should be able to take that to the bank. In fact, oftentimes that's what people end up needing to do. They make plans based on your assurance, they spend money based on your agreement, they put in their two weeks after you said the job was theirs. They tell *other* people that it's set, that's happening, that it's a done deal.

When we say that a person's word is their bond, that's in part what "bond" is referring to. Not just a tie between two people, but a literal deposit. A contract.

A handshake should be enough. Your word should be enough.

Because where are we if it's not?

In the 1960s, the young poet Diane di Prima was at one of those legendary Beat parties that movies are made of. Everyone was there. There were drugs and ideas and romances. Jack Kerouac was there, Ginsberg too. And yet di Prima got up to leave and go home early to relieve her babysitter.

Some of the other writers in the room found this laughable, believing that the literary life must take precedence over such pedestrian matters. "Unless you forget about your babysitter," Jack Kerouac said to her in front of everyone, "you're never going to be a writer."

Yet di Prima left anyway. Being a good parent and a good writer, at their cores, required the same thing, "the same discipline throughout." She had to keep her word. To her work, to her family, every time she made a commitment.

Don't let anyone tell you different. Don't let anyone judge you for that.

We should not pretend that this is always going to be easy. Living up to that vow—the one about sickness and health, about faithfulness until death do us part? That will test you. You told your family you'd never drink again, you told the voters that if elected . . . but now you have to hold yourself to that, come hell or high water. Promising to help a friend move is one thing, but what about keeping a promise to a friend who has broken their end? Paying back someone whom you dislike? What about an agreement that has gotten a lot more expensive, that is now liable to really upset people? Lawyers might be involved. Threats might be made. Uncertainties will loom. Reciprocity might well be laughable if the shoe was on the other foot.

It's natural to experience doubt. It's natural to hope it resolves itself, or even to ask for grace or latitude. To want an exception or a pass. But in the end, there should be no escaping a word freely given and taken, a contract signed in good faith.

You said it, they're counting on you, *do it.* Even if it doesn't seem like a big deal. Even if it's going to be difficult or painful.

We will regret many things in this life. But we'll never regret *being the kind of person* who keeps their word.

Who swears truthfully with their actions the promises they made with their mouth.

Tell the Truth

~

Cynthia Cooper alerted the world to one of the largest accounting frauds in history. Daniel Ellsberg exposed the secret history of America's war in Vietnam. Tyler Shultz helped bring down Theranos. Dr. Li Wenliang spoke up about a devastating virus emerging from China, the one his country wanted to cover up.

For this, they have become known as "whistleblowers," but what they did was much simpler, much more basic.

They told the truth.

They saw something. They said something.

Ernie Fitzgerald, who exposed cost overruns and $500 hammers and $7,000 coffee makers in his civilian role at the Pentagon, saw it this way. He didn't like the label "whistleblower," preferring instead to be called a "truth-teller." He preferred to see it as what he was paid to do as an employee and expected to do as a citizen. His wife, Nell, agreed. On the night before he was to testify before Congress, with his bosses pressuring him to play dumb, she told him, "I didn't really think I could live with a man I didn't respect and if he went over there and lied, I'd have no respect for him."

Whistleblowing is an aggressive form of truth-telling, speaking up with a twist of personal or professional risk. It becomes necessary when one has discovered a lie or a fraud, when one has witnessed or been the victim of some foul deed that the world does not know about. You'd think that this kind of courage would be appreciated, but it isn't. While we sometimes come to respect and admire whistleblowers long after the fact, more often than not they are doubted, pressured, criticized, and attacked.

Their motives are impugned. Their personal lives are scrutinized. Even with considerable legal protections for whistleblowers—which in the United States dates back to 1778—this act of public service is not an easy one.

Ernie Fitzgerald's reward for committing his act of truth? He became the most hated man in the air force. Secret recordings caught Nixon telling his aides to "get rid of that son of a bitch" and then had him fired. It's a reminder that for all the lip service we pay to the truth, in fact, honesty is often a radical, even dangerous act. It may well be one of the rarest things in the world.

How many truly honest people do you know?

People who tell the truth even when it's inconvenient? Who make it clear where they stand? Who don't equivocate?

Could you honestly put yourself in that category?

"The simple act of an ordinary brave man is not to participate in lies, not to support false actions!" the Soviet dissident Aleksandr Solzhenitsyn would explain. "His rule: Let that come into the world, let it even reign supreme—only not through me."

The politician blusters and exaggerates about something insignificant—the size of a crowd—and gets the people around them comfortable with being at odds with the facts, with their consciences. Hitler did this, cowing his generals into accepting his insane lies, long before he had killed a single person. At Theranos, investors and employees alike understood that there was a big gap between the reality of their products and the marketing, telling themselves that this was part of the Silicon Valley hype machine. But lots of money depended on them pretending otherwise.

It's not always this dramatic. We put overly optimistic projections in our pitch. We buff up our résumé. We dance around the unpleasant answer, we let omission do the heavy lifting. It's a bit of a journey from "fake it until you make it" to outright fraud, but not as far as you think.

We didn't want to lose our access. We really needed their support. Other people do it way worse! We choose not to see . . . so we don't have to say or do anything. *It's for a good cause.*

We always have our reasons.

There is the old fable about the emperor who had no clothes

and the sycophants who didn't want to tell him. In real life, the emperor Hadrian lorded over a court filled with such people. It was why he saw so much potential in a young boy named Marcus Aurelius, who was drawn early to philosophy and who always seemed to say what he thought, even to the powerful. Hadrian nicknamed him Verissimus, which meant the "the truest one."

Marcus Aurelius, later emperor himself, came to despise those who could not be honest as a policy. Particularly grating to him were people who would begin a remark by claiming they were going to give it to him straight, implying, as we all so casually do, that most of the time we're not doing that. Honesty should not need a preface. An honest person should be like a smelly goat in the room, Marcus would say—*you know when they're there.*

An honest person keeps their word. They don't hide behind jargon. They don't sneak around. If there's going to be a delay or a problem, they'll tell you. If they have concerns, they'll voice them—they won't nod their head, only to say "I told you so" later. They don't fool themselves with wishful thinking or the desire to be well received. They accept that, like Cassandra or the messengers in *Antony and Cleopatra*, they won't always be believed or appreciated.

Not that they're a jerk about it. There is a distinction between telling the truth and attacking people, between saying what you think and giving people your unsolicited opinions about how they should live or look or act. "Speak the truth as you see it,"

Marcus Aurelius reminded himself, "but with kindness. With humility. Without hypocrisy."

The truth hurts enough by itself. You don't have to try to be hurtful.

Which brings us back to the whistleblowers. Often they are accused of seeking attention or trying to make themselves famous. This is laughable, because they have almost always attempted to first politely, privately address what they have discovered. They have exhausted every internal (and official and unofficial) channel, sometimes over the course of *years*. They have given their bosses all due respect. They tried to keep the laundry in-house, trying to clean it instead of washing it in public. It was only after this failed—after every good-faith effort was rejected—that they sought the attention of the media or the law.

But ultimately, they did what they had to do. They didn't shy away from that either, because they knew it was right.

They followed the timeless advice that the poet Juvenal gave a Roman politician named Ponticus, back in the second century AD:

Be a good soldier, a good guardian, an incorruptible judge; if summoned as a witness in some dubious and uncertain case, even if the tyrant Phalaris himself should command you to life, and bringing up his bull, to dictate the perjury he would have you to tell, count it an abomination to prefer life to honor, and to lose for the sake of living, the reason to live.

In matters big or small, public or private, convenient or inconvenient, whether it will be rewarded or punished, tell the truth. Be a bastion of truth in a time of lies. Say *not through me.*

It is not just the right thing to do, it is your job. As an accountant. As an officer. As a receptionist. As a spouse.

As a human being.

Take Responsibility

~

A teenage Maxwell Perkins, the future editor of Ernest Hemingway and F. Scott Fitzgerald, was swimming with a friend in New Hampshire. As they swam across a small, deep pond, the other boy, Tom, began to drown. Panicking, struggling, Tom grabbed his friend's neck, pulling him down under the water.

Perkins, a strong swimmer but by his own admission a timid and cowardly kid, fought to break free and made it almost all the way back to the shore. But something in him, something other than the scared seventeen-year-old inside him, took over and he splashed back toward Tom. Managing to grab his friend right as he went under, Perkins swam them back, exhausted, to shore. Out of the water, he cleared Tom's airway and saved his life.

As kids with close calls often do, the two swore to never speak of the terrifying moment again. But it changed Maxwell Perkins forever. "I then made the only resolution that I ever kept," he would later tell a friend. "And it was, never to refuse a responsibility."

It is the first decision one makes in a life built around justice.

We evade responsibility because it's hard. Because it comes with risks. Because we have a tough enough time taking care of ourselves. Because we'd rather someone else be responsible. But what kind of world would it be if everyone did this? If no one would pick up the resolution that changed Perkins's life?

Certainly not a very just one.

Before we can take responsibility for the life of another, we must begin, as Joan Didion famously said, by the decision to take responsibility for our own. It is from here, she said, that *character* and self-respect stems. The most basic decisions about our conduct—deciding what kind of person we're going to be— are not just matters of discipline but also of justice.

Will we handle our shit? Or do we expect someone else to?

Are we someone who can be counted on? Or not?

Are we someone who does a great job . . . or the minimum?

Do we care about the consequences of our actions or just our own self-interest?

Who we choose to be affects more than just us. It ripples out into the world.

Realizing this is not just clarifying but deeply empowering. What we do matters. *We matter.*

While this might feel a little egotistical, it is certainly preferable to the immaturity of the alternative—which the vast majority of people choose—which assumes that very little is serious, that the stakes of everything are quite low, that one can continue indefinitely in their state of arrested development.

There is a beautiful statue dedicated to liberty in New York City's harbor. There is no such monument to responsibility. That's something we have to look inside ourselves to find.

We might not have signed the social contract, but each of us inherited it. Each of us is bound by its obligations, its duties, its expectations.

"The phrase 'I am not responsible' has become a standard response in our society to complaints of a job poorly done," Admiral Hyman Rickover once pointed out. "This response is a semantic error. Generally what a person means is, 'I cannot be held legally liable.' Yet, from a moral or ethical point of view the person who declaims responsibility is correct: by taking this way out he is truly not responsible, he is *irresponsible*."

The world is filled with these types of people. People who don't care that they said they'd do something. People who are only honest if they think somebody's watching or if they'll get in trouble. People who fritter their gifts away, thinking they have unlimited time or multiple lives to lead. People who never stop to think about how their decisions affect anyone else. People who are weak and incapable of doing anything for themselves or others. People who step back, assuming someone else will step forward in their place.

Each of us has been like this at one time or another—because we were young or little was expected of us, because no one called us out on our immaturity, because life had been easy and we were not tested. There's a part of us that fears that responsibility will put a crimp in things, that it won't be fun. Or that there is something inherently unfair about having to assume it since so many people clearly do not.

Maxwell Perkins, after he saved that boy, would go on to be one of the greatest editors in the history of literature. He would do his best to help great talents reach their potential, to make possible the expression of their incredible genius. He would also be responsible for them, the adult in the room while they often acted like children.

One cannot help but see echoes of this relationship in Fitzgerald's short story "The Adjuster," which Perkins edited in the mid-1920s. The story centers around a woman named Luella Hemple, a wealthy young wife who has more or less skated through life. She is bored and entitled, indifferent to her new baby, overwhelmed when the servants leave to her even the simplest task. She fantasizes about getting divorced so she can go off and go back to having fun.

But then, suddenly, a series of tragedies. A series of responsibilities and realities. Spinning from all of it, she's helped by a mysterious doctor who tells her she must step up and be an adult.

"We make an agreement with children that they can sit in the audience without helping to make the play," the doctor tells her as they sit on her couch, "but if they still sit in the audience after they're grown, somebody's got to work double time for them, so that they can enjoy the light and glitter of the world."

"But I want the light and glitter," Luella protests. "That's all there is in life. There can't be anything wrong in wanting to have things warm."

"Things will still be warm," the doctor reassures her.

"How?"

"Things will warm themselves from you."

And then the doctor delivers to his stunned patient a definition of justice that Rickover would have approved of, one that we must each aspire to if our lives are to be aimed at it. "It's your turn to be the centre," he said, "to give others what was given to you for so long. You've got to give security to young people and peace to your husband, and a sort of charity to the old. You've got to let the people who work for you depend on you. You've got to cover up a few more troubles than you show, and be a little more patient than the average person, and do a little more instead of a little less than your share. The light and glitter of the world is in your hands. . . ."

"It is your turn," he tells her, "to make the fire."

We think it would be wonderful if we didn't have to do this. If we could simply break free of the things that try to pull us under, if we could go on staying in the audience or being the child, if we could say, "I am not responsible."

But this is not possible. It is a lie.

We are responsible.

We are burdened but also privileged now. Because from this responsibility comes meaning and purpose—comes intense, life-giving warmth.

Which is why we must swear never to refuse it.

Be Your Own Referee

W hen he connected with the ball, Frank Robinson was positive that it was going all the way over Fenway's left-field wall. So positive, in fact, that he ran at half speed to first base watching the ball soar deep, deep toward the netting above the thirty-seven-foot-tall wall affectionately known as the Green Monster. Then suddenly the ball came up short, banging off the concrete and tin and ricocheting down to the waiting left fielder.

Robinson, usually a fast runner, had to settle for a single in what might have been a double or a triple had he hustled.

In the end, his Orioles won in a blowout, so it didn't seem to matter. A mistake easily forgotten, but one of some ten thousand at-bats in his twenty-one-year career. Except that afterward, Robinson walked into the manager's office and slammed down $200 on the man's desk.

He was fining himself.

He hadn't broken any league rules, but he had given less

than his best. More important, he had violated a central tenet of baseball's culture—that you run out every hit—and his failure had cost the team.

He wasn't going to wait for someone to say something. He didn't care that they'd won. He didn't care if they'd let him get away with it. He did the crime, he was going to do the time—or in this case, pay the fine.

It doesn't matter that we had a good reason. Or if it worked out all right in the end. We have to hold ourselves to a high standard, higher than perhaps even the organization itself. And we have to be brave enough to willingly accept the consequences when we fall short of those standards, in fact, calling them out even when nobody notices.

That's what makes someone an MVP (in Robinson's case, in both the National and American Leagues, and a World Series MVP to top it off). It's also how he bound teams together, as an athlete and as a manager—by modeling and never exempting himself from a culture of rectitude and rules.

There's what they'll let you get away with and there are the standards you hold yourself to.

Yes, courts and public opinion are important. No one would be able to play sports without a rulebook and referees and leagues who enforce those rules. These are important institutions that play an essential role in leveling the playing field and making the world fair. But before and beyond all that, there is the justice that's up to us, what we enforce upon ourselves. This is what really counts.

Not everyone chooses to see it like that. Look at the controversial career of the golfer Patrick Reed, who is undoubtedly successful and incredibly wealthy, yet he has also been dogged his entire career with accusations of cheating and rule-breaking. "If you take what you think is a correct drop, and it turns out to be an incorrect drop, that's a rules infraction, and there's a penalty. Happens all the time," Reed once said, trying to explain away another scandal. "Cheating is intentionally trying to gain something on the field."

Look, when you're making distinctions between cheating and rule-breaking, you've already lost . . .

Sure, let's say that cheating can help a person get ahead, but to *where*? Are you sure you're going to like where it takes you? Being honest, holding yourself to account, can you hold you back, sure—but it only holds you back from shame. Honesty prevents you from having to keep secrets or hoping you don't get exposed. It makes you great in the way that Frank Robinson was great, greater than winning or losing the game (and in no small way it also helped him win a lot of games).

In 2012, the Kenyan runner Abel Kiprop Mutai became confused at the end of a long race and pulled up a few meters short of winning. The Spanish runner Iván Fernández Anaya, close behind, could easily have used it as a chance to win. Instead, he gesticulated, ultimately pushed his competitor ahead—thus losing his own chance to win.

Yet they both won, in a way, and so did everyone watching, by being and seeing humanity at its best.

In ancient Greece, there was a Stoic named Chrysippus, who was also a runner. He, like competitors today, wanted to win— he wanted to win badly; that's what sports and life is about. But he also understood that without a sense of honor, without a commitment to rules and fairness, victory is meaningless. "It is not wrong to seek after the things useful in life," he said, speaking of the laurels that go to the champion as well as the spoils of success in business or politics, "but to do so while depriving someone else is not just."

Letting the cashier know that they forgot to ring you up for something, letting the customer know that you overcharged them, pointing out to the ref that they made the wrong call to your advantage . . . it's not free to do this . . . but freely paid, it's better than being a free rider. Better than being a cheater.

No one would know but us . . . but that's who counts, right? That's who you have to look at in the mirror at home.

In the months-long battle of Vicksburg in the Civil War, General Grant and General Sherman disagreed about Grant's proposed plan of attack. Sherman, thinking the plan was too risky, advised against it in writing. To his surprise, Grant's strategy was a stunning success. A few days later, at Sherman's headquarters, Grant found Sherman speaking to a group of Northern officials who had come to celebrate the victory. "Grant is entitled to every bit of the credit for the campaign," Sherman told them without solicitation. "I opposed it. I wrote him a letter about it." And when, years later, he heard that Grant had destroyed the records, Sherman sent his copy to Grant's biographer so that history would show his friend had been right.

It doesn't matter if you could get away with it, because that doesn't get you anywhere. It doesn't get you anything worth having.

So we call the penalty on ourselves. We don't accept "freebies." We pay our own way . . . we pay our taxes gladly. We'll gladly give someone else a break, but we're much stricter with ourselves. Out of an abundance of caution, we'll flag it. We'll disclose the conflict of interest and recuse ourselves. We'll issue the correction. We'll call the judges over. We'll plunk down the fine even if the coach didn't ask. If we're wrong—or if someone claims to have been wronged—we'll apologize.

Our lawyers will tell us this is crazy (think of the liability!). Our accountants will be confused. Our fans will be outraged. Our spouses or friends will be puzzled. Our competitors will lick their chops.

We may lose because of this . . . but we won't lose what's important.

We'll win what really matters. We'll win the right way.

Good, Not Great

~

Long before he became one of America's greatest novelists, Walker Percy was a struggling medical student. In 1940, making average grades at Columbia, he wrote to his then dying uncle, William Alexander Percy, for advice.

This was a family with a long and intimidating legacy of success. Walker Percy expected a lecture. He expected shame. At best, maybe he hoped for some encouragement ... or money for a tutor. Instead, his uncle Will, who had adopted Percy and his brothers and introduced them to the writings of Marcus Aurelius and the Stoics, told him he did not care for *one second* about the grades.

"My whole theory about life," Will wrote back, despite the fact that he himself had effortlessly graduated from Harvard, "is that glory and accomplishment are of far less importance than the creation of character and the individual good life."

Marcus Aurelius himself faced some version of this. He was young and talented, selected for great things at an early age. As a result, he could have vied with Alexander the Great for conquest. He could have tried to build more than Augustus. He could have tried to be more brilliant than Cicero, to have more fun than Tiberius.

He had the resources. He had the brains. He had the power.

But he didn't care about any of that.

Meditations, a notebook of reminders and motivational sayings he wrote to himself, is not filled with plans for becoming famous. Or accomplishing things. Or trying to beat other people. Instead, over and over again, it focuses on something much humbler, much more internal. "Remind yourself that your task is to be a good human being," he writes, "remind yourself what nature demands of people. Then do it, without hesitation." Cribbing from Plato, he tells himself to concentrate on one thing and one thing alone: *to do what is right and to behave like a good man.*

Not winning battles.

Not making money.

Not making his mark.

But doing good, being good. Being fair. Being decent. Being honest. Being dependable.

"A better wrestler?" Marcus wrote to himself, perhaps noticing how much energy he was putting into training in the sport he loved. "But not a better citizen, a better person, a better resource in tight places, a better forgiver of faults?"

A better parent, not a better professional. A better teacher, not a better *taker*.

The poet Hesiod noted how the carpenter competes with the carpenter, the singer with other singers. It's the energy that drives the world forward, but rarely makes people better. We seem only to vie with each other for professional success, not for kindness or civic-mindedness, for fame, not friendship.

But what would it look like if more people decided to try to see . . .

. . . who could be the most trustworthy?

. . . who lived a more ethical life?

. . . who helped the most people?

. . . who could forgive the most grievous wrong?

. . . who prevented the battle instead of won it?

. . . who had the smallest carbon footprint, not the biggest house?

. . . who raised the kindest kids, not whose got into the best college?

The Spartan king Agesilaus tried to live that way, measuring himself against other rulers not by wealth or fame or the beauty of his bride, but by who was more just. What was even the point of being a king, he once said, unless he could be the greatest and most fair of all his contemporaries?

There are lots of talented people out there. People who can do and have done incredible things. They break records on the field. They make discoveries in the laboratory. Their businesses employ thousands. Their art dazzles us.

But when it comes to what kind of people they are . . . well, suddenly they're not so unique. They're a run-of-the-mill asshole. Another shark. Another backstabber. Another hypocrite. Another walking cliché. Another cautionary tale.

There is an old aphorism: *It's easier to be a great man than a good one.* Certainly there are more of the former than the latter.

Justice is greatness, but it's a different kind. The people we admire for conduct, for their decency—these people aren't doing these things to get ahead. More often than not, these standards *cost* them as much as they help them. Which means they're doing it for a very different reason.

Each of us has to make a decision right now about where we are going to put our efforts, what we're going to work toward. Because what a person measures, goes another expression, gets managed.

Epictetus, the slave whose philosophy so influenced Marcus, dismissed competition to achieve the highest rank or the biggest fortune or the most beautiful skin. These are superficial, meaningless metrics. "Is there nothing in a man such as running in a horse, by which it will be known which is superior and inferior?" he asked. "Is there not *modesty, fidelity, justice?* Show yourself superior in these, that you may be superior as a man."

This will take a serious recalibration. Because it's simple to compare bank balances . . . but how do you quantify integrity? Field goal percentage is straightforward . . . but what about being a good teammate? Elected leadership is about who got the most votes . . . but what gives one the moral authority to *lead*?

The decision to opt out of the former races for the latter (or prioritize one over the other) is a decision that takes courage. But it is a decision rooted in justice, that makes the world a better place. Virtue has to be our compass, goodness has to be our goal.

This will take as much work as mastering any profession. It will require sacrifice too—it will be painful (in the short term) to become the person you want to be.

And the good thing about being good is that you can do it *any* profession. In fact, there is no profession where this is not impressive, not important, not imperative.

In the end, it should be noted that Marcus Aurelius did achieve great things (as did Walker Percy). He was courageous on the battlefield (as was William Alexander Percy). There still stands in Rome a forty-meter tower in marble detailing Marcus's achievements . . . just a few blocks from a grand equestrian statue of him. But what is he doing in this statue? Raising his arm to pardon the barbarian tribes that had battled Rome. He holds no weapons, he brings with him not war but peace. By focusing inward, he made his mark externally. The man who wrote in *Meditations* that doing the right thing today was far more valuable than posthumous fame managed to get both.

This is more than irony. It is the point.

He was good for so long that he became great.

History is replete with ambitious, successful people. Decency, honor, kindness, we see much of this. To be good and good at what you do? This is more than rare.

It makes you a unicorn.

Be an Open Book

~

The Rome that Marcus Livius Drusus lived in was not an honest or an honorable one. As a young man, he watched his uncle, the Stoic Rutilius Rufus, driven into exile by powerful interests for *not* taking bribes. The courts were a farce, the political process even more of a joke. Rome's oligarchy had all but given up any pretense of legitimacy and lapsed into indulgent luxury.

The system looked like it was collapsing, and political violence was commonplace.

Into this mix stepped Drusus, the inheritor of enormous wealth, the head of a powerful political legacy. He could have been corrupt like all the rest. He could have debauched himself like all the rest.

Instead, he built a reputation on being the opposite. As a politician, he was a reformer. He fought for expansive citizenship rights. He expanded the Senate. He tried to resolve class conflicts. As a private citizen, he was so generous it was said that all that was left to give was mud and air. He was clean, he was respected.

One day an architect came to Drusus with an offer. Noticing that Drusus's home was partly exposed to public view, the designer proposed some simple measures that would allow the man some much deserved privacy.

"Double your fee," Drusus replied, "and make my whole house visible, so that every citizen may see how I live my life."

The word we have for this today is "transparency," and sadly, very few powerful men or women seem to think they are obligated to practice it. Not only do they live in mansions between high walls, surrounded by guards, but they hide their businesses between shell corporations and tax havens. Our politicians refuse to disclose their income or conflicts of interests. They meet in secret. Their publicists spin and deflect. Their lawyers obscure and protect.

Why?

So they can get away with stuff, of course. So they can keep prying—that is, *judging*—eyes away from what they know would not go over well with the public, with their investors, with the law.

"There is not a crime, there is not a dodge, there is not a trick, there is not a vice," Joseph Pulitzer famously said, "which does not live by secrecy." Or as the Bible put it, evil *hates the light.*

While there is nothing wrong with being a private person, the truth is that by going into business or politics or leadership or art we have chosen to be *public figures.* Not famous but *public,* in the sense that we serve and are responsible to someone or something other than ourselves. What we do, how we conduct ourselves—this matters.

In 1630, when John Winthrop spoke of America as a "city on a hill," he wasn't speaking of American exceptionalism. He meant it as an admonition. That a city on a hill can't hide. That the world was watching and that this new country—built around virtue—needed to be a good example.

The decision to live and work with transparency serves as a kind of immunization against corruption, dishonor, or dishonesty. No doubt, many laws have been passed to help make this decision easier. Public disclosures. Quarterly reports. Proxy statements. Insider trading reports. But as we've said, justice is more than this. A transparent person doesn't just act in compliance with the law but goes out of their way to give their stakeholders the information they need. They don't hide the ball. They give it to you straight. They definitely don't lie or deceive.

Still, this is only a start . . .

Who cares what the health code obligates you to disclose? Your customers deserve to know what's in the food they're eating. Who cares if you don't *have* to keep your investors informed? They trusted you with their money and they should know how it's being spent. Who cares what *most* companies or professionals do? Just because your profession doesn't mandate an ethics policy doesn't mean you can't make one and be public about it. Just because you can get away with opaque contracts or hidden fees doesn't mean it's right—that doesn't mean we should.

Don't wait to get caught. Don't hope the problem will escape notice. And on a more personal level, don't string people along—be upfront about your needs and plans.

There is the story of a Spartan king who met two of his subjects, a youth and the youth's lover, accidentally in a crowd. Embarrassed, the subjects tried to hide their blushing cheeks, but the king noticed and replied, "Son, you ought to keep the company of the sort of people who won't cause you to change color when observed."

If it makes you ashamed, if you wouldn't want to be seen, you'd dare not do it in public, if you leave it only for the night ... what does that say?

Imagine the changes we would see if more of life was subjected to this test. If businesses were proud of how their products were made and what their supply chains looked like. If customers could stomach where their food came from. Even if some people didn't care (or complained because things cost more), it would still be the right standard to hold ourselves to.

That fact that we're so outraged when someone isn't transparent with us should be enough to demand from us that we be more transparent than we might like to be.

Each of us will have to decide what transparency looks like in our industry or life and how much transparency makes sense.

But each of us can make a commitment to be as straightforward and transparent as we can be, to try not to do anything that, as Marcus Aurelius said, "requires walls or curtains." This is transparency not as a marketing ploy or a meaningless buzzword, but a way of living, a conscious choice to embrace the light, to let it cleanse you and illuminate your example for others to see and follow.

Thomas Jefferson knew this. In 1785, he wrote in a letter to his friend Peter Carr that "whenever you are to do a thing tho' it can never be known but to yourself, ask yourself how you would act were all the world looking at you, & act accordingly." Great advice . . . that he knew he was woefully short of following. There in Paris, where he wrote this letter, Jefferson was joined by Sally Hemings, his slave and concubine, whom he controlled and raped (and strung along with hopes of freedom . . . and of legally recognizing their children).*

In recovery circles they say that we're only as sick as our secrets. Jefferson was a man sick with secrets, compromised by the horrors of slavery that his people covered up and lied to themselves about. Which he himself was disgustingly complicit in. He did not act like all the world was watching, not with his affairs nor his conniving against his boss and colleagues as a

---

*And to prove Pulitzer's point, it was a journalist who first broke the story of Jefferson's shameful affairs in 1802.

member of Washington's cabinet. He thought he could get away with it and he did it.

But now that we know? Well, we don't think so much of him anymore.

At the very same time in the very same country, Ben Franklin was explaining that he wouldn't need to fire his valet if it turned he out was a British spy—as he suspected he was (and he in fact was)—because Franklin, like Drusus, tried to live in a way that was above reproach.

Meanwhile, how many of our marriages would survive our spouse looking at our phone? Or our boss seeing what's in our email? How many reputations would survive a lawsuit that made it to discovery?

If we're inclined to hide it, we probably shouldn't do it. If we dread the publicity, maybe we're not living or doing right.

We should strive for the opposite. We *want* people to see what we're doing. We *want* to be the city on the hill. We should be the kind of person who the more they hear about us, the more they respect and admire us.

Let us live in a way that makes us proud. Let us act during the day in a way that allows us to sleep at night.

Be Decent

~

The famed lawyer Clarence Darrow was traveling by train along the Pacific coast when he and his son had a bad experience with a steward. The line snaked through the dining car. Passengers grew impatient. The underpaid staff seemed to be interested in helping only those who could afford to tip them, and everyone was upset with each other.

"Will you report him to the Chicago and North Western when you get back?" his son asked about one rather rude waiter, knowing that his father had contacts at the railroad from years of representing the owners. "No, no, son," his father said, brushing off the slight. "Never hurt a man who is working for his living."

How distant and traditional this seems compared to our world, where flight attendants are assaulted by passengers and we take every lost package as a personal affront. It's a sad fact that staff dread the Sunday brunch rush, when even customers straight from church seem to have no problem treating service staff like garbage.

The idea that the people who wait on you or work for you are deserving of respect? We'd agree in theory, but if someone listened to the recordings of the calls we made to customer help lines, they'd doubt our sincerity . . . and our decency.

In his later years, Darrow—needing the money—was hired to do a speaking tour where he would debate other personalities onstage across the country. He was contracted for $500 per event with $50 for his expenses. But then he heard after the first debate that the promoter was clearing barely $150 after costs and speaker fees.

That wasn't fair and he wouldn't have it.

"That's not enough," he told the man, "you forget the expense money and take a hundred dollars from my check in addition." Later in the tour when the profits had risen, Darrow still kept himself only to his original fee, forgoing thousands of dollars of the proceeds. "Mr. Darrow always leaned over backward to give men the best part of the deal," his partner explained with awe.

To Darrow, it was just the decent thing to do.

Part and parcel of justice is the understanding that other people are sovereign individuals with dignity and value, and that because of these things, we must treat them well. Respect is justice. It's something everyone deserves.

Whether they're important or not, how we treat them says everything about *who we are.*

In those heady first hours after becoming president, Truman

had a lot on his mind. The load of hay had fallen on him . . . and yet he wasn't thinking about himself at all. His first thought was for Mrs. Roosevelt, whom he allowed to stay in the White House as long as she needed (and as we said, asked her what *she* needed from him). The second thought was for his neighbors in his $120-a-month apartment on Connecticut Avenue, who he was concerned might be flooded with unwanted attention and noise by having a president next door.

How we treat people in ordinary circumstances is one thing. How we treat them when we're tired, when we're stressed, when the weight of the world is on our shoulders . . . when someone has just screwed up, just cost us something serious. This is everything.

During the pandemic, this was a test that so many of us failed. Not just the people who couldn't be bothered to take basic precautions for other people, to think about how their actions affected other people, but also the rest of us, who were quick to write off those people—forgetting that they themselves were victims of misinformation, of stress and fear and totally unfamiliar circumstances, which in some cases claimed their lives too.

"It seems ridiculous," Albert Camus wrote, "but the only way to fight the plague is with decency." This is true for every disaster and enemy and situation: The way to beat it is to prove yourself superior to it, to not let it change your values, to not let it devalue other people, even as the tragedy or virus does precisely that. Decency, he said, "helps men rise above themselves."

People who didn't know Truman, like Churchill, marveled at his decision-making. The people who knew Truman were much more impressed by his decency. His relationship with his mother-in-law was the prime example. She had repeatedly tried to discourage him from marrying her daughter, yet after the wedding, she would live with them for the next three decades. He never once complained. He never once responded to her digs or disrespect. In the political fight of his life, his mother-in-law asked why Truman was "running against that nice man Mr. Dewey." He smiled and let it go. He was kind to a woman who was repeatedly unkind to him.

He didn't cheat in business, politics, or on his wife. He was decent to the people who worked for him. "If a fella can't be patient and considerate of the people who are actually doin' the work for him," he once said, "then he's not any good, and I don't like him."

And "not yelling" is only the lowest bar. Who do you think has to clean up the mess you leave behind? Who do you think carries all that baggage you brought with you? Who has to run all over town to get that thing you asked for? Sure, the boss is entitled to change plans—but are they aware that this means someone else has to call their spouse and cancel that anniversary dinner?

That this means someone else has to work harder, longer, under more stress? Nice words are great . . . raises are better.

Sticking up for the little guy is not just empathy, it should also be a point of honor. *I don't cross picket lines.* It's also good strategy. When you treat everyone with respect and interest, as if they could do something for you, you'll be amazed to find out that they can. And will! You never know who will end up as the editor of *The New York Times,* or who will pass by your car later as you are stranded by the side of the road. Everyone has something to teach us. Everyone is a future voter or customer or patron. Fortune is fickle, we never know when we might find ourselves the little guy.

That you were tired is not an excuse. That they didn't treat you well isn't either. Nor is the fact that you're under a lot of stress. If Truman could find a way to be decent to people, if people racked with pain or grieving a spouse manage, so can you.

In a world of awfulness, of injustice, of cruelty and corruption, ordinary decency stands out. Miep Gies, the friend who ran errands for Anne Frank's family as they hid from the Nazis, said that these small acts of friendship, of honesty, of kindness are like turning on a small light in a dark room. It's something anyone can do. It's something that makes a big difference, that reverberates and illuminates more than we might think.

People are having a hard time out there. Let's not contribute to anyone's burdens. Let's try to lighten them when we can.

Other people want the same things we want. Dignity. Security. Respect. Freedom. Happiness.

We might all look different and live very different lives, but we should remember that all of us feel pressed for time, feel inadequate or insecure. Let's treat people accordingly.

Let's do what we can. Let's be a small light in a dark world.

Do Your Job

~

He was a southern good ole boy. He'd never gone to college. He had been a police chief in a small Alabama town at the height of segregation. And he had known John Patterson, the state's racist governor, since he was in third grade.

So when the governor had ranted about and tried to stop the Freedom Rides—which attempted to integrate buses across the South in 1961—everyone had expected him to toe the party line. "There's my public safety commissioner," Patterson told the representative of the Justice Department, "his name's Floyd Mann and he can't protect them. Tell him, Floyd."

With that, Floyd Mann took a deep breath and made the most momentous statement of his life. "Governor, I'm the commissioner of safety," he said. "If you tell me to protect these people, then I'll protect them." And then Mann proceeded to lay out the most ambitious protective detail offered to protestors in the history of the nascent civil rights movement—highway patrol in front and behind the integrated buses, helicopters and airplanes above, with a reserve of highway patrol cars ready at the first sign of trouble.

The room was stunned, and nobody more so than the governor. The only person who didn't find this strange at all was Floyd Mann, who seemed to actually take seriously the duty of his position, which was, after all, *to keep people safe.* While the Justice Department and those brave Freedom Riders had notions of equality and societal transformation on their minds, Floyd Mann was thinking of a smaller kind of duty. "My purpose was law enforcement," he later reflected, "trying to make sure nothing tragic happened to those people while they were in Alabama."

It's a powerful thing, isn't it? When someone does their duty? When they take their job seriously—even in the face of private pressure or public opprobrium. When they put the details aside, when they say, *As long as I have this authority, wear this coat, bear this license, or wear this badge, I am going to do what's right.*

It says something about the world today that the phrase "I was just doing my job" is more likely to be an excuse for disturbing behavior than to be the explanation of heroic behavior. It's a way of letting yourself off the hook when really what a job, what a duty, is all about is what it demands of you, from you.

The writer Yuval Levin, despairing at the decline in so many of our precious institutions, spoke of the need for each of us to force "ourselves, in little moments of decision, to ask the great unasked question of our time: 'Given my role here, how should

I behave?'" That's what people who take an institution they're involved with seriously would ask: "As a president or a member of Congress, a teacher or a scientist, a lawyer or a doctor, a pastor or a member, a parent or a neighbor, what should I do here?"

What he's talking about is *duty*. Not what's convenient. Not what's easy. Not what everyone else is doing but *what we are obligated to do* as a result of our potential and talents, as well as the profession or roles we have selected for ourselves in the world. In business, they talk of the duty of a "fiduciary," meaning that once one has taken on a role of responsibility—to a company, to investors, to the customer—they can't simply do whatever is best for themselves. In a famous case in New York in 1928, Chief Judge Benjamin Cardozo ruled against a partner who had attempted to enrich themselves at the expense of another partner. "A trustee is held to something stricter than the morals of the marketplace," he wrote in his decision. "Not honesty alone, but the punctilio of an honor the most sensitive, is then the standard of behavior . . . the level of conduct for fiduciaries [has] been kept at a level higher than that trodden by the crowd."

Some duties, like that of a fiduciary, are codified in the law. Some are defined and enforced by a strict professional code, like in journalism. Others, like the role of a soldier, are a combination of both. Unfortunately, most jobs and professions are not so clear. Or worse, the professions have abandoned their duty.

Was Pontius Pilate doing his job as a magistrate when he sent

Jesus to be crucified? Yes, it's true, his job was to judge cases, and in some of those cases, mete out the strict punishments of Roman law. But Pilate also knew that Jesus was innocent, remarking several times that he could see no offenses in which Jesus had actually broken the law. Still, he sentenced him to die because that's what the mob wanted—because it was the most expedient choice. He knew this, literally telling the crowd that he washed his hands of the matter, that the blood was on their hands as he turned over his job to them.

The job of the police officers in Alabama was to "protect and serve" people—not do whatever the governor told them. Certainly the governor had ditched his responsibilities, deciding to surf public opinion rather than enforce his constitutional obligations. Meanwhile, the local police in cities the riders traveled through were collaborating with the KKK to target the activists.

Such was the scene in Montgomery, where a racist mob—encouraged by the police—attacked the riders with a ravenous, deadly anger. As a young John Lewis disembarked, he was besieged and beaten, watching helplessly on the ground as his friend, Jim Zwerg, was almost killed. As he attempted to reconcile himself to his own impending death, two shots rang out.

One man marched forward through the surging crowd, undeterred even as his clothes were nearly torn from his body by frenzied, fleeing attackers. He knelt beside a white man murderously slamming a baseball bat into a helpless victim, put his gun against the man's skull, and said calmly, "One more swing and you're dead."

It was Floyd Mann.

The riot ended right then.

"Seest a man diligent in his business?" reads the Bible verse. "He shall stand before kings." In that moment, Floyd Mann, a public servant with a rather boring title, was every bit the hero and king. Of course, he had no sense of that as he did it, no fantasy of riding into the rescue or capturing the limelight. It was something much simpler and earnest, a friend would later reflect. The man thought he was "doing his job the way a good lawman ought to."

The man had sworn an oath. It didn't matter that it was dangerous. Or that it was unpopular. He was going to keep it.

Sometimes doing your job requires extraordinary measures. Other times it's very ordinary—but it's always heroic. We should learn to recognize equally not only the journalist willing to go to jail to protect their source, but also the journalist doing their day-to-day job, insisting on objectivity and fairness, resisting the temptations of clickbait, speaking *truth* to power. It's not John Adams representing the British soldiers involved in the Boston Massacre, it's every lawyer representing any client, even the guilty ones. It's not just Helvidius defying the emperor Vespasian in the Senate, or Harry Burn's vote to ratify the suffrage amendment at the cost of his political prospects, it's your ordinary local official putting party aside and doing the people's business. It's not just Galileo refusing to turn his back on science, but also Dr. Katalin Karikó studiously working in her underfunded, underappreciated laboratory for *decades* as she pioneered the mRNA research that would develop the COVID-19 vaccines. Her job was to keep doing her job—even when her bosses left and she had to reapply for her job time after time, even if recognition and appreciation were hard to come by.

We do our job whether it's recognized or appreciated because we signed a kind of oath when we took it. We signed a contract. We put on the uniform. They paid us money. Now we have to hold up our end of the bargain.

Sometimes our job will place us in situations of life or death, like Floyd Mann. Sometimes they involve the big news events of their time or huge scientific breakthroughs. But they can also be much more ordinary. Saving lives, battling evil, these things are important, but so is deciding not to be a dishonest or unreliable contractor. Or an inept bureaucrat. To decide to actually give your all to the teaching profession, to leave no child behind, even as your hours are extended and your salary frozen. To zealously represent a defendant you can't stand. To be an athlete *and* a role model.

Maybe this doesn't seem that hard, but it's rare enough that we know that it is.

Professionalism. Duty. Commitment. Putting the citizens,

customers, audience, patients first. And not just in our chosen line when everything is wonderful, but when the chips are down—when the line's a razor's edge.

This makes you extraordinary.

When we do this, when we do our job, we are helping not just the people in front of us but society as a whole. We are elevating that standard. It's true, maybe nobody will notice. Maybe it won't make a difference. Maybe you won't get credit. Maybe you'll even piss your boss off. But? The alternative should be unthinkable.*

If your profession doesn't have a code of ethics? *Make one.* To not have one is a recipe for moral dilemmas, for slip-sliding, if only unintentionally, into gray areas. How could you possibly do right if you don't know what right is? How could you possibly do your job well if you haven't defined it?

Some jobs are lofty. Some are quite lowly. "Each has his or her place in the procession," Walt Whitman once wrote. But do we play it well? Do we fill it credibly? Do we bring honor or shame to it? That's on us.

There is in fact a guideline for each and every profession. "What is your vocation?" Marcus Aurelius asked himself. It wasn't just ruling the empire or writing philosophy books, just as yours isn't just making more money or getting the paperwork

---

*And it should be said, if they ask or expect you to do something that is wrong . . . it is not your job.

out on time. It was something simpler and more basic. "To be a good person," he said.

So it goes for you. Your job is to be like Floyd Mann, whatever that happens to be in your chosen line, in your troubled times. Keep the people safe. Show up. Be honest. *Care.* Act like a fiduciary. Even if you aren't legally obligated to be one, you must obligate yourself to a standard higher than the one trodden by the crowd.

You swore an oath to yourself.

Now keep it.

Keep Your Hands Clean

⌒

"Here," a cop in civilian clothes told Frank Serpico one afternoon in a parking garage. "I have been holding this for you."

It was an envelope with $300 in it.

"What'll I do with it?" Serpico asked.

The cop was surprised. "Do anything you want," he said.

And there it was—out in the open at last. The plausible deniability gone. The unspoken temptation for every person in any position of power suddenly made real, in the form of a wad of old tens and twenties.

He had been handed a bribe.

Would Serpico, a beat cop trying to make detective, take it? Would he get dirty like the rest of them? It'd be easier if he did. The path not to wasn't even clear. Who could he tell? Even if he threw the envelope away, did it change the fact that someone had handed it to him—and the person who had provided it now expected something?

The story of Frank Serpico reads like fiction, but it is all too real and all too timeless. It was his decision to not be paid off, to not be corrupted, to risk his job and his safety to go public with it that is all too rare.

But for the rest of us, corruption is usually much more subtle.

No one asks us to rob a bank, and rarely do they throw an envelope of cash at us, but they may ask if we want anything for ourselves when they've got access to the company expense account. They don't put a gun to our head, but they do a very vivid job of letting us know how much support we'll lose if we take a certain stand. They show us how much easier it would be, how it's simpler this way. They shrug and say, "Don't we deserve it?"

There was a group of wealthy Romans who grew tired of Cato the Younger's moral compass. So they connived to get him a job in a distant province of the empire known for its shady dealings and access to pleasures and luxuries. "You will come back from there a far more agreeable man and more tame," one of them predicted to Cato. They weren't trying to bribe him explicitly, they just wanted expose him to *how things were supposed to be done.* They wanted to desensitize him a little.

We have to resist that. Just because everyone else does it a certain way doesn't mean it's the right way. Just because it's the way it's always been done doesn't mean we should go along with it. Just because the offer seems harmless, or is done without pressure, doesn't mean that they're not trying to corrupt us, not trying to mess with our moral compass.

It's the scene in *The Great Gatsby* where Gatsby tries to approach the young Nick Carraway, whom he needs to win back the love of his life. "I carry on a little business on the side, a sort of sideline," Gatsby tells Nick. "And I thought that if you don't make very much . . . this would interest you. It wouldn't take up much of your time and you might pick up a nice bit of money. It happens to be a rather confidential thing."

Years later, Carraway, understanding more clearly that Gatsby was a gangster and a bootlegger, comes to see that "under different circumstances that conversation might have been one of the crises of my life." Gatsby was trying to draw him into that life—not cruelly, but because he was hoping to ask him a favor later. But Carraway, sensing that the offer was "obviously and tactlessly for a service to be rendered," cut him off and claimed to be too busy.

We all tell ourselves it won't affect our judgment. Why shouldn't we make a little money on the side? *Nobody will get hurt . . .*

It was not a surprise that Patrick Reed betrayed the PGA Tour to take an enormous greenwashing contract from LIV, a Saudi-backed competitor. He didn't care about being above suspicion when it came to the rules, so why would he care where his money was coming from? Why would he care about how his decision affected the game—or other up-and-coming golfers?

What he and the other golfers who jumped ship (and then

tried to bully their old league into letting them keep their old privileges too) wasn't illegal, but it was pretty gross.

Rory McIlroy, on the other hand, turned down hundreds of millions of easy dollars because he thought that the new league was bad for the game. A decision "you make in your life purely for money doesn't usually end up going the right way," he explained.

What did he get for this loyalty? For the victories the distraction of it all cost him?

The PGA Tour and its commissioner in turn betrayed him, attempting to merge with the very league that weeks earlier they had implicated in the horrible attacks of September 11, 2001. (You could say he got off easy. Frank Serpico was suspiciously shot in the face in the line of duty after blowing the whistle.)

Trying to keep your hands clean earns you enemies. Your decision implicitly rebukes theirs. And they may be stronger, craftier, or more vicious than you. But what matters is that at the end of the day, you comported yourself with dignity and self-respect.

"In all this long career, I had certain rules I followed, win, lose or draw," Truman explained. "I refused to handle any political money in any way whatever. I engaged in no private interest whatever that could be helped by local, state or national governments. I refused presents, hotel accommodations or trips which were paid for by private parties . . . I made no speeches for money or expenses while I was in the Senate. I lived on the salary I was legally entitled to and considered that I was employed by the taxpayers, and the people of my country, state and nation."*

This meant that he didn't have much of a fortune to pass on to his daughter, he admitted, but he was passing her something he believed could never be stolen, "an honorable reputation and a good name." It was her job, as it is all of our jobs, not to spoil that heritage.

No one is saying you have to be a saint. Just try not to be a sellout. Try not to be "dyed purple," as Marcus Aurelius reminded himself, speaking of the emperor's cloak and the way the job seemed to change the people who wore it. Try to honor your code, your commitments, your conscience. Beware of the gray areas. Beware of the false promise of "just this one time." Try to avoid temptations, try to ignore what other people around you are doing. Try to be at least *cleaner* than average. Cleaner

---

* It should be noted that Admiral Rickover, whose command set up the title of this book, was implicated in a scandal at the end of his sixty-three-year career for supposedly receiving gifts worth a few thousand dollars from military contractors (most of which he passed on to politicians and people who worked for him). Considering he had stayed in the navy at great expense to himself and regularly oversaw budgets worth many, many millions, money and perks were clearly not what he was after. Still, it was this lapse in judgement that gave enemies a chance to hurt him. That's why we must keep our hands clean.

than the people who came before us. Cleaner than we were yesterday.

Captain Arthur MacArthur—the father of Douglas MacArthur—was serving in New Orleans after the Civil War. There, a cotton broker trying to win the use of some army facilities left a large cash bribe in the hotel room of the young officer. MacArthur took the money and instead of keeping it for himself sent it to the U.S. Treasury. "I request immediate relief from this command," he wrote to his superiors. "They are getting close to my price."

You gotta know your weaknesses and make decisions so you can be strong.

Because if we don't, we'll get ourselves into real trouble. The first time we see it, we're horrified. New sailors on slave ships reacted with horror. The same goes for executives touring a sweatshop. Or the prison guard. The first taste of illicit money. But the third or the fourth time? After a while on the job? It just becomes part of the job. Our conscience is dulled.

Few of us can deal in filth without becoming dirty. Very few of us can compromise without being *compromised.*

When Cato returned from Cyprus, he faced a Rome that was willing to compromise with Caesar, even as Caesar violated Rome's norms. They thought they could work with Caesar, use his energy for their purposes. This was a dangerous bargain, Cato warned. They were putting Caesar on their shoulders, he said, but would eventually lose the strength to carry him . . . or put him down.

The same goes for whoever's water you end up carrying—for money, for access, for an opportunity to get ahead. Or whatever you're turning a blind eye to. A person gets comfortable. We find out that we did have a price.

And then we pay the ultimate price.

Because that's the kind of person we are now.

Integrity Is Everything

I n 1935, Martha Graham got the opportunity of a lifetime—she was invited to present her work at the forthcoming Olympics. It was dance on the world stage, the kind of opportunity that no talented or ambitious person could afford to turn down.

Yet there she was, turning it down.

"Three-quarters of my group are Jewish," she told the emissaries from Berlin. "Do you think that I would go to a country where they treat hundreds of thousands of their coreligionists with the brutality and cruelty that you have shown Jews?"

Shocked that self-interest had not been enough, that she wasn't interested in looking the other way as everyone else they asked had been, the delegation of Nazis tried a different tactic. "If you don't come," they told her, "everyone will know about it and that will be a bad thing for you."

But Graham knew it was precisely the opposite. "If I don't come," she replied, "everybody will know why I didn't and that will be a bad thing for *you*."

She may have been a starving artist, well into her forties at that point, and could have used the money and the exposure. But it was not worth her integrity. It was not worth her soul. And by acting by her principles, she was striking a public blow against an evil that not enough people had yet condemned.

"Integrity is one of those words which many people keep in a desk drawer labeled 'too hard,'" Admiral James Stockdale would reflect after his time in the Hanoi Hilton, the infamous North Vietnamese prison.

And it is very hard!

As F. Scott Fitzgerald points out in another one of his stories, with a character choosing between blowing up his Wall Street career or doing right by some poor farmers on the other side of a business deal, "People talk of the courage of convictions, but in actual life a man's duty to his family may make a rigid course seem a selfish indulgence of his own righteousness."

Despite his role as the architect of the Union victory in the Civil War, Ulysses S. Grant's relationship to slavery was a complex one, as it was to many Americans at that time. Grant was raised in a free state and his father had been an ardent abolitionist, but his wife had grown up comfortably on a plantation worked by slaves. Then there were the economic realities: Grant had bounced out of the army, and he was supporting his family by selling firewood on the side of the road, trying to eke out a living on an eighty-acre parcel called Hardscrabble.

At the rock bottom of his finances, going from military captain to dirt-poor farmer, Grant suddenly came into possession of a slave named William Jones, probably a "gift" from his wife's family. Grant's long unease with slavery could no longer be avoided—slavery was no longer something other people did, or something he indirectly benefited from. *He* was the owner of another human being.

It was an injustice Grant simply could not stand. Even though it was the lifeline he had prayed for. Even if it was a way out of his humiliating, backbreaking poverty. On March 29, 1859, Grant made the costly choice to give William Jones his freedom. We can imagine Grant trying to explain to his wife how he had freed a slave "worth" $1,000 because he couldn't stomach selling him, her watching as the exhausted and broken West Point grad trudged back out to his fields.

It was just one person, hardly a dent in a system that enslaved some four million men and women and children at that time, but that didn't change what it would mean to that one person. It also meant something to Grant, though he could hardly afford to linger on it. He needed to get back to work, honorable—if excruciating—labor compared to wringing bread from the sweat of another man's brow.*

Integrity is living by what you think is right. Not what you can get away with, not what everyone else is doing.

For the most part, it's not illegal to sell stuff to dumb people

---

* Like with Lincoln, Grant's views on the legality of slavery would continue to evolve until the Civil War.

who don't know any better. In only a handful of cases is breaking your word a crime. In fact, in America, lying—even egregiously so—is protected by the First Amendment. But just because we *can* doesn't mean we *should*.

Each of us has competing obligations, views, incentives in life. We will be presented with dilemmas. We will find ourselves in vexing moral quandaries, presented with temptations, the logic of a given situation. Stockdale certainly knew this. He was a father, he was a citizen, he was an officer—he was a person trying simply to *survive* in the heinous, torturous world of a POW. He was beaten. He was also offered a chance to make all that pain go away, if he would just help his captors . . . and himself out. "A person's integrity can give him something to rely on when his perspective seems to blur," he explained, "when rules and principles seem to waver, and when he's faced with hard choices of right or wrong. It's something to keep him on the right track, something to keep him afloat when he's drowning."

There is an expression: It's not a real principle *unless it costs you money.* Integrity ceases to be an abstraction when life presents you the opportunity to act on it. Integrity then becomes real. It is proven. You have proven yourself responsible and responsible to it.

But it doesn't just take from us. It also guides us, supports us, reassures us.

The philosopher Agrippinus was once approached by a man who had been invited to one of Nero's famous banquets. He was thinking of attending, as bad as Nero was, because he didn't want to make any enemies. What did Agrippinus think? Go for it, Agrippinus said.

But you're not going, the man replied. That's right, Agrippinus said, "*For me? I do not even raise the question.*"

Integrity had already answered it for him.

How could Graham have looked her Jewish friends in the eye, then and later, when the true horrors of the Nazi regime came to light, knowing that she had lent her name to a propaganda effort? Grant didn't have much going for him in those wilderness years, but he knew his hands were clean. They might have been callused and blistered, but they were clean.

That's what Joan Didion said about self-respect—which is what integrity is rooted in. To be without it, she warned, "is to lie awake some night, beyond the reach of warm milk, phenobarbital, and the sleeping hand on the coverlet, counting up the sins of commission and omission, the trusts betrayed, the promises subtly broken, the gifts irrevocably wasted through sloth or cowardice or carelessness."

A life of integrity will cost you. It will be difficult.

And yet somehow we all know that to live without it is the worst fate of all.

When we see others pull ahead of us because they have acted without it, when we see them bending the rules or taking bribes, we must remember where that road ultimately ends.

Integrity may sometimes be relegated to the drawer labeled "too hard," but life is much harder, much sadder without it.

Realize Your Potential

~

On a frigid night in Chicago in 1927, the architect and inventor Buckminster Fuller decided to end it. He was a failure. He had been kicked out of Harvard. He had buried a child. His drinking problem was a secret shame.

It was time, he thought, to swim out as far as he could into Lake Michigan and drown.

Yet as he prepared to die, he heard a voice, a voice that said in effect, *How dare you? Who do you think you are—to abandon the responsibilities of life? To your children? To the world?*

"You do not have the right to eliminate yourself," the voice said, "you do not belong to you. You belong to the universe. The significance of you will forever remain obscure to you, but you may assume that you are fulfilling your significance if you apply yourself to converting all your experience to the highest advantage of others. You and all men are here for the sake of other men."

He carried this thought with him back from the ledge, and indeed, for the rest of his life. The work he did, the inventions he created, the children he raised were an attempt to fulfill that obligation, that he wasn't here on this planet for himself, but to be good and do good for others.

It's almost too perfect that the story in the Bible about three servants, each left with an amount of money by their master, is known as the parable of the *talents.* One servant, skilled and able, by investing, turned five talents (a very large sum) into ten. The second servant, more slowly than the first, was eventually able to do the same. The third, overwhelmed by the whole proposition or not interested in participating, simply buried his in the ground for safekeeping.

The true moral of the story is about what we do with the talents we've been given, what we make of ourselves and the opportunities before us.

Some grow. Some hide. Some reach their potential. Some don't.

And this is a matter of justice.

Just as the servants owed it to their master to make a return on the money he had entrusted them with, just as Buckminster Fuller owed it to whoever gave him life to do something with it, we owe it to our master—*to the world*—to make the most of the skills and abilities that we each have. Without people who did this, where would we be?

There would be no progress. No greatness. No art. No innovation. No bravery on the battlefield. No social change.

Florence Nightingale was born with all that potential. She had an education. She had wealth. She had access. But for many years—sixteen, in fact—she was like that third servant. She hid underground. She let her parents and her fear of what they would think paralyze her. She averted her eyes from her destiny, could not find it within herself to answer the call. The world was worse off because of that, just as it is worse off when *any* person settles or cowers.

But with time and encouragement, she did venture out. She broke her shackles—finding that the ties that bound her were but straw—and in the process broke through centuries of bad medical practices, saving the lives of millions of soldiers around the world.

Yet each of us ignores this call in our way, if not outright, then in the way that Jimmy Carter did—a man whose life was shaped by his early reading of the parable of the talents as much as it was by the intervention by Admiral Rickover, who asked him pointedly why he hadn't always given his best. When we don't do our best, when we hold something back, we are cheating ourselves. We are cheating our gifts. We are cheating the potential beneficiaries of us reaching our full potential.

To whom much is given, the lesson from the parable goes, *much is expected.*

That doesn't mean money and success, necessarily. "I can very well understand how you feel that to be anything less than the greatest in your line would be failure," Uncle Will wrote to Walker Percy in that letter. "I used to think the same way about poetry," he explained of his own writing. "But now I do not regret having written it, although what I wrote does not rank with the greatest and may well be forgotten shortly. If I had thought this would be its fate, I would not have written, but now I am glad I did. It was the best I could give and if it is not the best somebody else could give, that is not my concern."

Do your best. Become what you can be. You owe the world that much.

It makes a difference, even if others are indifferent to it: People who realize their potential employ other people, they inspire other people, open doors for other people, discover and make things of use for other people, create markets for other people, have a platform they can use to speak to other people. The decision to participate in this system—for yourself and thus for other people? This is a moral choice.

If you don't agree, then consider the alternative. A system that crushes the incentives to fulfill one's potential. A world where people *don't* participate. They *don't* care. They *don't* try. How many breakthroughs don't happen? How much change doesn't happen? How much needless suffering is there?

"Whoever could make two ears of corn or two blades of grass upon a spot of ground where only one grew before," wrote Jonathan Swift, "would deserve better of mankind, and do more essential service to his country than the whole race of politicians put together." Yet the same holds true for any kind of leader. The one who makes an agreement where no one saw a possibility, the one who restores faith instead of breaks it, who fully realizes the potential of their office or their powers—this is a person who is bringing about a small amount of justice in an unjust world.

And in fact, one of the most basic principles of economics is the *law of comparative advantage*. If one of us is better at growing corn and the other at growing grass and a third at the art of politics, then we best serve the world by seeing to that specialty. By doing what other people want us to do, or think we should do—or by lacking the discipline to keep the main thing the main thing—we are *costing* the world something.

Angela Merkel was a very talented scientist, but with time she came to realize that talented scientists were more common than talented politicians. Like Merkel, like Nightingale, you have unique gifts and advantages. Like President Carter, you have within you a level of performance and commitment that is deeper than what you have so far given. What will you do with this? What will you make of it?

Oscar Wilde believed that each human being was a prophecy, that we had a destiny. Our job, he said, was to fulfill it. As he would write in *The Picture of Dorian Grey,* "The aim of life is self-development. To realize one's nature perfectly—that is what each of us is here for." Yet too many people, he wrote, like that third servant, were afraid of themselves, of the task they had been given.

Will you become what you're meant to be? Will you go where you are most needed?

That is the question.

To fail to answer it because you're afraid is a betrayal of your gifts. It's shortchanging the world.

Especially when we consider that it's possible to have an even more ambitious goal than just *realizing* our potential. Because that word implies that each person has only a finite amount of it. What if it's possible to do even more? We should try to realize the things that nobody thought were possible, that nobody would have expected of us. More than doing our best, we should strive to become our best, to vie with the best. *A man's reach should exceed his grasp . . .*

Certainly that reaching, that stretching is what gets us closer to heaven.

But down here, still on earth, what you don't want, what people should never find themselves needing to say about you, is the most damnable indictment there is:

They could have been more.

They could have done more.

They *wasted* their gifts.

Be Loyal

~

The reason that Truman and Eisenhower had a falling-out wasn't because of anything Eisenhower had done to Truman. In fact, Eisenhower hadn't done anything. That was the point.

Eisenhower, like many of America's best military officers, had been mentored by General George Marshall. Marshall had, for decades, kept a little black book of names of men whose careers he wanted to help advance, which he did tirelessly to the benefit of the free world. So much so that in 1943, when FDR offered Marshall, then chief of staff of the U.S. Army, the opportunity to command Allied forces for the invasion of Normandy, Marshall turned it down so that the job could go to his protégé . . . a gesture whose selflessness was topped only by the fact that he took the time to send an original copy of the presidential orders to Eisenhower as a memento and congratulations.

Given his undisputed role as the architect of the Allied victory in World War II, few could have predicted that just a few years later Marshall would be repeatedly slandered by Senator Joseph McCarthy, who baselessly claimed that Marshall was a communist and a traitor. In a speech before the Senate in 1951, McCarthy placed Marshall at the center of "a conspiracy on a scale so immense as to dwarf any previous such venture in the history of man."

It was insane. It was cruel. It was also popular and widely believed.

At a campaign stop in Wisconsin in 1952, Eisenhower had a chance to do something about that. "I know him, as a man and a soldier," Eisenhower planned to say in defense of the person to whom he owed his career, "to be dedicated with singular self-lessness and the profoundest patriotism to the service of America." But the governor of Wisconsin, concerned it might cost Eisenhower the state's electoral votes—and concerned it would also be awkward given that McCarthy was sharing the stage— begged Eisenhower to let it go.

All he had to do was say a few words—words already written—on behalf of a great man he knew well.

Instead, chose to do nothing.

It was more than a failure of courage, it was a stunning moment of disloyalty. After all Marshall had done for his country, and done for Eisenhower personally, here he was, abandoning for political calculations, compromising, Truman would say, "every principle of personal loyalty by abetting [a] scurrilous big-lie attack."

He could never see Eisenhower the same way. How could Eisenhower—an otherwise brave and decent man—leave Marshall hanging like that? How could he live with himself?

The answer is the same way that we all do it.

By not even thinking about it at all. By telling ourselves nothing that can be done. By telling ourselves that they'll understand . . . because they'd do the same thing in our position. By telling ourselves it's for the greater good.

We put the small town where we're from in the rearview. We break away from the people who discovered us now that we're big shots. We leave a friend hanging because they're radioactive. We ditch a longtime supplier when someone offers a few pennies of savings.

We rationalize the knife as it goes in. We turn our eyes away and let someone else do it.

Loyalty is expensive. It's inconvenient. It gets in the way. It's messy, it's complicated, it's hard to explain.

For years, America was riled up and riven by McCarthy's Red Scare. Many innocent people lost their jobs and reputations. Relationships were torn apart, ties were cut—preemptively, self-protectively. Nobody wanted the heat or the trouble—and if you found yourself in the crosshairs, it was your own fault . . . and everyone for themselves.

There were also, it happens, a few actual spies flushed out into the open, one of whom may have been Alger Hiss, first accused of passing secrets to the Soviets but ultimately brought up on perjury charges by an ambitious congressman, Richard Nixon.

We talk today about "cancel culture," but Hiss was facing federal prosecutors, a potential death sentence for treason, and the inescapable social and professional death that controversy brings. Even though the evidence against him was hardly airtight (and in retrospect, anything involving Nixon and J. Edgar Hoover warrants skepticism), the charges were as serious as they get.

Yet remarkably, Truman's secretary of state, Dean Acheson, stood by Hiss, a longtime friend and former colleague. "I will not forsake him," Acheson said to his wife on the morning he was to give his weekly press conference. The press pool, sensing a major story, naturally asked Acheson about Hiss. Acheson said all the safe things—that the matter was before the courts and it was inappropriate to comment on a pending legal matter. He could have stopped there, neutral, noncommittal, *no comment.*

But Acheson would not, as a matter of honor. "I take it that the purpose of your question was to bring something other than that out of me," he told reporters. "I should like to make it clear to you that whatever the outcome of the appeal which Mr. Hiss and his lawyers may take in this case I do not intend to turn my back on Alger Hiss."

And while this statement was as shocking to Acheson's political opponents—who believed Hiss a traitor—as it was moving to his friends, what really mattered was what the president thought. The thing about loyalties is that we never have just one of them—our obligations are layered, and occasionally in conflict with each other. We are loyal to friends, but we also owe loyalty to our family, whom we have to provide for. We are loyal to someone for whom we've worked for a long time, but we also owe a loyalty to our work, to our cause, which is at risk of being jeopardized. Acheson's duty to his friend was real, but did he not also have obligations to his office, which represented his country? To Truman, at whose pleasure he served?

So Acheson made his way to the White House, fully expecting that he might have to once again hand an American president his resignation. Truman would have none of it. "He looked at me," Acheson would reflect, "and said he understood why I had said what I said." Truman told him the story of attending Tom Pendergast's funeral and explained that what mattered, what people would remember, is that somebody stuck by their friends. Then Truman looked Acheson in the eye and said, "Dean, always be shot in front, never behind," and told him to go back to his office. "We've got a lot of *important things to do.*"

Truman believed in loyalty, even when it cost him. That's why he went to the funeral, even though he suffered politically for it. He was also loyal to his fellow citizens and the taxpayers, which is why he declined any of the opportunities for corruption that Pendergast may have slyly passed his way. He didn't hedge his loyalty either—Truman could have just sent flowers.

He was *out front* with it, not lagging, not hoping for a safe opportunity. And it's why he stuck to Acheson as he stuck to Hiss, even if Hiss may well have been profoundly disloyal himself.*

Would you want a president who wasn't loyal? Would you bet your franchise on an athlete who sees the whole business as transactional, has no affinity for the city or the team? Would you want to invest your money with someone who leaves people hanging because helping them would be inconvenient? No, you wouldn't.

Life is hard. Loyalty is complicated! (What if Hiss was guilty? Should Acheson have forsaken him then?) No one said it wasn't, nobody said friendship was all take and no give. Many potential whistleblowers have kept themselves quiet out of loyalty or love for the institutions that they serve—debating whether their obligation was to a person or to an organization . . . or to the truth. Nor should we skip over where loyalty can leave us—game theorists speak of the "sucker's payoff," which was perfectly expressed by Seneca when he said that "loyalty provides the disloyal man access to do harm."

It's true. And?

We don't control what other people do. We don't control whether we live in a time of mob justice. We don't control the

---

* Hiss would maintain his innocence until his death in 1992. Evidence revealed after the fall of the Soviet Union was not favorable, but his actual guilt remains debated.

fact that these decisions are agonizing and complex and that there is no guidebook. We control what *we do.*

We have to make the call, own it, even if that means getting shot in the front instead of safely lurking in the back. We can't be the quiet Eisenhowers—knowing what we should say or do, what feels right, and then declining at the last minute, not wanting to invite the heat.

No, we have an obligation . . .

. . . to the people who helped us

. . . to the places that made us

. . . to those who have been loyal to us

. . . to the truth and to our cause

. . . to the downtrodden and besieged and the friendless.

We can't wash our hands. We can't stand on the sidelines. We can't abandon ship.

We don't have to condone what they did. Loyalty does not mean protecting people from the consequences of their actions. Still, the person who is in the middle of watching their life fall apart is a person we should be sympathetic to—that we should, if not clothe and feed, at least send a nice note to. Even if we're disappointed or even angry with them. Even if they did wrong. We can at least call and see how they're doing. When everyone else is turning away, we lean in. When everyone else starts thinking of themselves, we refuse to betray our commitment.

We can love them as a person, even if we hate what they did.

It was in the middle of one of these scandals that one of Truman's advisors tried to be pragmatic with the president. "You've been loyal to people who have not been loyal to you, Mr. President," they said.

It was true. But that's sort of the point.

Loyalty is something we give. It's not something we expect.

Nor is it something we ought to expect to always be understood.

We do it because it's right.

Choose a North Star

~

At one point, the fashion mogul Dov Charney owned the largest garment manufacturing operation in North America, producing some fifty million garments a year. The average garment sewer globally then made somewhere less than fifty cents per hour. Charney's American Apparel regularly paid as much as $20 along with health benefits, subsidized lunches, and transportation.

Investors were confused. It didn't make any sense. If he moved the factories overseas, the business would be enormously more profitable. There would be less oversight. He'd actually, in some cases, have access to better technology and more workers.

But Charney had a reason. "I didn't get into this business just to make as much money as possible," he would constantly explain. "If all I cared about was profit, I wouldn't be in this business at all. I'd have become a drug dealer."

Charney wanted to make money, of course, but that was not his north star. He cared about the thousands of garment workers he employed, choosing to treat them well, providing them with health and retirement plans instead of grinding them down in a sweatshop overseas (which were not only legal but the unquestioned standard practice of the fashion business). He cared about the environment. He cared about political issues. He cared about artistic expression.

Or at least he did for a time.

Which is what makes Charney such a fascinating and tragic figure. For years, his commitment to something higher than his own self-interest actually served his interest quite well, making him rich and famous and beloved. Workers cheered him as he walked the floors of his factory. The business press celebrated him as a genius.

But with time, this goodness went sour and was replaced by—or competed with—his ego, his resentments, his need for control, his illicit affairs and lack of discipline. In the process, he would not only crash and destroy the business he had built, but he would be one of those heroes who lives long enough to see themselves become the villain.

Such is the power of a north star. Such is the power of values. They are, like discipline, a kind of destiny.

Or a curse.

Either way, they foretell a prophecy. They determine where we'll end up . . . and who we'll be when we get there.

Discipline can feel constraining, like it's telling you what you can't do. Justice is something different. It is an ideal to aspire to, something higher to aim at. That's what a north star is.

Something to reach toward. Something beyond the horizon, lifting our gaze up instead of down.

It cuts through the noise. It solves the dilemmas. Of the cardinal directions, justice is clearest—it points us north, shows us where to go.

The weather will change. But the stars do not.

For Truman, his commitment was not simply honesty or fairness, but it was those values for a reason, and the reason was because that's what a politician owed the public they served. His north star was the American people and the American Constitution that had been written to secure their rights. His north star was that ancient idea of virtue that he'd learned as a boy, and it rooted and directed him even in the darkest and stormiest of times. He once quoted the poet Horace from memory: "The man who is just and firm of purpose can be shaken from his stern resolve neither by the rage of the people who urge him to crime nor by the countenance of the threatening tyrant."

Isn't that what you want?

For Queen Elizabeth II, for more than seven decades, her north star was not the British Empire that she inherited but the British *Commonwealth*—the association of fifty-six nations across the globe—to which she dedicated her life. For Martin Luther King Jr., it was nonviolence—which he said he took as his "lawfully wedded wife"—in the pursuit of justice and love in the world. For Regulus, it wasn't just personal honor that he sacrificed for but the integrity of Rome and her security. For whistleblowers like Ernie Fitzgerald or Cynthia Cooper, it wasn't just escaping liability or complicity in various crimes—or advancing their careers—but about informing the public who *deserved to know* what was happening in their name or to their money.

It was to these causes that they gave the best years of their life. It was these causes that provided clarity amid chaos. It was for these causes that they both refused to compromise . . . and were willing to make any compromise to bring about. Their why allowed them to bear, as the saying goes, just about any how.

Of course, the same talents, the same people would not be nearly so impressive if they had taken their bearings by self-interest, by ego, by a desire for revenge or domination or pleasure. As the writer Budd Schulberg observes in his classic novel about drive and character, *What Makes Sammy Run?*:

> What a tremendous burning and blinding light ambition can be where there is something behind it, and what a puny flickering sparkler when there isn't.

Cash is a bad north star . . . but an easy one to default to if you don't have anything better. Ego. Fame. Power. Dominance. These things might lead you to the top . . . but they will also lead you astray. They corrupt. They corrode.

Loyalty. A love of the game. A desire to keep your hands clean. The confidence to compete fairly with the best. Integrity.

The Greeks had a word, *pleonexia*—self-serving—which they said was the worst kind of life. We might say that justice, virtue—being *good* and not just great—is the antithesis of this. One takes you north, the other south, one leads you forward, the other backward, down, down to depths.

When Charney followed his conscience, he did great things. When he followed his lower self, he was a monster. He would lose everything, but even if he hadn't, if the law and justice had not come for him? Still, he would have been the loser because he had lost his way.

So it goes for all of us.

Are we going to be perfect? Get it right every time? Doubtful. We will lose our bearings in this life. We will be tempted off the path. We won't always be as certain as Agrippinus. But when we falter, when we get lost, we can look up at that celestial point. We can check in with our conscience.

Follow it, and we'll get where we need to go.

Right Thing, Right Now

~

> There can be only one way to fight the general evil of life: It is in the moral, religious and spiritual perfection of your own life.
>
> —LEO TOLSTOY

We often know what the right thing to do is. The problem is timing. Is this the right opportunity? The right moment? To a person of integrity, though, the right time is obvious.

Jimmy Carter won a surprise victory for governor of Georgia in 1970. At his inauguration in 1971, however, he had another surprise in store. After a conservative campaign in a conservative state, there he was, minutes into his term, stunning everyone by announcing, "I say to you quite frankly that the time for racial discrimination is over."*

Admiral Rickover had tried to teach Carter that the right time for the right thing was *always right now.*

---

*As governor, he said, "I will not shirk this responsibility."

"It's impossible for me to delay something that I see needs to be done," Carter later explained.

Discipline is so often a battle against procrastination. But justice can be too. We don't want to do it because we know it will be hard. Because we know there will be costs. Because we have other priorities too. The tricky thing is we don't have to tell ourselves we're *never* going to do it, we can tell a comforting lie instead: *I'll do it later. I'll do it when I'm more secure. I'll do it when it will really count.*

But this violates Aristotle's view of virtue. It wasn't a thing you arrived at, it was a daily practice—it was a habit. And in this daily practice, we become who we are.

. . . or not.

"You could be good today," Marcus Aurelius reminded himself, quite possibly as he was deliberating on some similarly controversial decision. "Instead you choose tomorrow."

The longer you stand out on the edge of a diving board, the harder—and less likely—it becomes for you to jump. You get in your own head about it. You come up with reasons. You lose your courage.

Let us not prolong our difficulties. Let us not shirk our obligations. Eventually, we'll have to do the right thing—make the changes, make the apology, make the hard decision, make the first move. So why not just get it over with?

We'll have to pay the price at some point. So let's start making the payments.

Not later. But right now.

PART II
THE WE
(SOCIOPOLITICAL)

Justice is the virtue that makes us useful to ourselves as well as to others.

—SOCRATES

It's not about you. It never has been. Discipline is a *me* virtue. Justice, one might say, is a *we* virtue. It's about the κοινωνικαί—the common good. It's one thing to be a person of personal rectitude, but what for? Because we want to make the world a better place. Because we want to contribute to the public benefit, as the Stoics advise. Because we care about other people—people who are like us, people we don't like, people we will never meet, people who are not yet even born. We come together to do good together. To do good for the less fortunate, for the struggling, for the persecuted, for those with different views, different needs than us. To be part of the solution and not the problem. To expand the definition of what's possible, what's solvable. To do for others what we wish had been done for us—and in so doing, do quite a bit for ourselves.

To You From Failing Hands We Throw the Torch . . .

~

It happened in May 1787. Twelve men gathered in a print shop in the heart of London. Some were Quakers. Some were Anglicans. Some were young. Some were old. Some were rich. Some were not. Some had a long history of activism, while others had never taken a public stand in their life.

For the most part, they were well-off, well educated, and had very little in the way of personal grievance, even direct familiarity with what they swore together to end: the transatlantic slave trade.

It was of course one of the most abominable institutions in the history of humanity. But it was also, in today's dollars, a multibillion-dollar industry. And for all its centrality to the economy, this terrible injustice was quite intentionally out of view of the average British person—there were no chains or whips or overseers in London. It all happened very far away.

Yet here these twelve individuals—all of whom had been born free—had decided to come together to tear it apart. It was as ambitious as it was seemingly inexplicable. Certainly, it was something quite new. As the historian Adam Hochschild would write, it may well have been the first time that "a large number of people became outraged, and stayed outraged for many years, over someone *else's* rights."

Is that true?

Even if it wasn't the *first* first time, it's still a moment that changed the world.

And as it happens, abolition began at a crossroads that Hercules would have recognized.

In 1785, two years before he would gather with twelve others in London, a young man named Thomas Clarkson entered an essay competition while he was a divinity student at Cambridge. The question was in Latin, as were all the essays: *Anne liceat invitos in servitutem dare?* Is it lawful to make slaves of others against their will?

Like many students, Clarkson's primary concern was his grade, and so he threw himself into writing what he thought would win, not taking much time to think about what he actually believed. It worked. His flawless Latin, his counterintuitive argument—that yes, the dominant view of their society was wrong, it was immoral to own slaves—brought him first prize and a rush of academic fame. Yet as he rode his horse away from the university, eager to enjoy the spoils of his promising new career, Clarkson found himself utterly preoccupied.

As much as he wanted to dismiss it all as some assignment, some classroom debate, he could not stop thinking about the argument he had made. *What if he was right?* What if it was wrong for one person to own, sell, or exploit another?

Dismounting to think, it came to be that he could not even keep walking his horse, so consumed was he by this question, which now rang repeatedly through his head. There, at a crossroads, in front of Wades Mill in Hertfordshire, Clarkson reached a life-altering, world-changing conclusion: If the contents of his essay were true, then "it was time some person should see these calamities to their end."

More directly, *that person could be him.*

In the end, it would take far more than just one man, far more than a dozen activists in a print shop too. It would be a truly multinational, multiracial, multigenerational coalition working together, working independently for over a century—until 1888 when Brazil became the last major nation to abolish slavery.

It would be nice to think it would have happened anyway, that society would have eventually just done the right thing. But there is something depressing, even disempowering about this notion, as common as it is. Because it eliminates the role that singular individuals—that people just like us—can have in the course of world events. It obscures what a man or woman with courage can do to bend the arc of history toward truth.

Or not do.

But in Clarkson's case, there was so much that needed to be done.

So much.

Clarkson began at the beginning. Not satisfied with his college-level understanding, he set out to actively study and research the institution most people refused to think about. He read everything about slavery he could find—how it worked, how profitable it was, what the people who worked inside it thought, what their secrets were. He interviewed slave traders and former slaves. He spoke to their insurance companies and port officials. He visited slave ships, boarding his first one on the Thames, going below deck and with "melancholy and horror" seeing the holding cells firsthand.

Working sixteen-hour days, traveling thousands of miles a month, he reviewed records and conducted interviews. He documented how deadly slave ships were, not just to the slaves but also to the crews—with as many as 20 percent of the sailors dying on each voyage. He gathered not just data but powerful stories that the public had never heard. He cultivated allies, befriending a freed slave and writer named Olaudah Equiano and later helping raise the money to purchase Frederick Douglass's freedom. He became close with the Marquis de Lafayette, inspiring him to pick up the cause, which Lafayette then helped spread in America and France for the next thirty years.

One of Clarkson's best recruits was a man named Josiah Wedgwood, a wealthy pottery magnate who worked for the queen. Wedgwood wasn't just convinced by Clarkson's arguments, he was able to translate them to the public in vivid imagery. It was Wedgwood who commissioned a logo for the group of activists, a drawing of a kneeling slave, clamped in wrist and leg irons, holding up his arms, begging for mercy. "Am I Not a Man and a Brother?" reads the banner at his feet.

It's impossible to conceive of how powerful this image would have been then, given that today we are children of the world it changed. We no longer question whether this lowly, pained slave is a human being, a brother to us all. But in the eighteenth century, this heartbreaking portrayal of the human costs of slavery hit people in the solar plexus, for the very first time disabusing them of many of the pleasant fictions that enabled their indifference.

Another, even more powerful image came shortly thereafter, a direct result of Clarkson's painstaking investigations. With sickening accuracy, he commissioned a drawing that detailed the exact specifications of a real slave ship, each of the slaves drawn by hand as they actually were crammed side by side under the decks. "The slaves stowed on the shelves and below them have only a height of 2 feet and 7 inches between the beams," goes the caption.

There it was, all laid out. The neatness and efficiency betrayed by the just barely visible facial expressions of each of the 454 men and women in the drawing. Slaves were not just laborers moved from one market to another, they were packed—worse than sardines—with industrialized greed in conditions that few living things could be expected to survive. Just as powerful photographs of a monk on fire or children in cages at the border can shift public opinion overnight, Clarkson's diagram went off like an explosion. No longer could the horror be denied or ignored. No one could possibly claim this was just or fair or decent.

But what could people do? Few had the right to vote in England, and certainly no slaves did. This was no accident. Powerful interests that benefited from slavery—as with any injustice—were not inclined to simply allow the people to legislate their profits away! It is the perennial problem of social movements—how do the voiceless use their voice to effect change?

The poet Audre Lorde would famously say many years later that "the master's tools will never dismantle the master's house." Yet with abolition, few quotes more widely miss the mark—and that's a good thing. Not just because Clarkson quite brilliantly collected the various tools of slavery—thumbscrews and chains and whips—which he then displayed to devastating effect at meetings or speeches.

Slavery was a product of capitalism, and capitalism would be used to kill it. Clarkson tied slavery to the institutions that depended on it, from textiles to coffee and tobacco. Most thoroughly, he went after the sugar manufacturers, a product inseparable from the brutal slave plantations of the Caribbean. "In every pound of sugar used," one famous abolitionist claimed, "we may be considered as consuming two ounces of human flesh."

It's not the kind of claim you want people to be able to make about your business!

A famous poet branded tea a "blood-sweeten'd beverage," and sales plummeted. Suddenly, one of England's most widespread cultural practices was connected to heinous cruelty. Turning teatime into a political act, Clarkson leveraged the publicity into the first effective consumer boycotts. Entire towns across England gave up sugar in protest, hundreds of thousands of people stopped taking afternoon tea—or switched to green tea instead. And it was more than just virtue signaling, as companies began to change their labor practices in response, announcing in their advertisements that their sugar was "produced by the labor of FREEMEN."

He had invented the political logo, the political poster, and the consumer boycott. He popularized the political petition and built the first diverse political coalition.* He used outrage to create cultural and, most significantly, legislative change. When Thomas Clarkson died at eighty-six in 1846, slavery had been

---

* The organization he founded remains in operation today, continuing to fight for the freedom of the oppressed, exploited, and trafficked.

dead in England for more than ten years, the slave trade for nearly four decades.

One man, one idea, millions of lives changed, untold suffering prevented.

A small group of committed individuals can in fact change the world, and they don't have to burn anything or anyone down in the process.

And yet this is only a fraction of their legacy.

Because shortly after Clarkson's death, while the fight against slavery in the United States still had many years to go, another group of people, riding the momentum of what abolitionists had begun, got together. This time, it was largely women, and a lot more of them—some three hundred in all. A little more than fifty years after the meeting in that print shop in London, this group met at a small chapel in Seneca Falls, New York. They had forgotten the key, but thankfully one woman's five-year-old son managed to sneak through an open window to let them in. There, at the Seneca Falls Convention, the women's rights movement— led by women who were all active in the abolitionist movement— was born.

"The history of mankind is the history of repeated injuries and usurpations on the part of man toward woman, having in direct object the establishment of an absolute tyranny over her," they declared, paraphrasing and improving on Thomas Jefferson with their own declaration. Their claims were not an exaggeration. Abigail Adams had in 1776 asked her husband to "remember the ladies" when the Founders drafted the laws for a new nation. Now, two generations later, women still could not vote and were forced to submit to a government they did not choose. Once married, a woman became "civilly dead," with no right to her own property or wages. They had no right to the custody of their own children. The best jobs were taken by men, and women expressly forbidden from them—from even attending schools where they might become qualified for these jobs. They could not sit on juries. They did not have control of their own bodies. They were held to a different code of morals and made to doubt their own value, their own powers and self-respect, to keep them dependent and at the mercy of their male counterparts.

Yet most of these women—accompanied in some cases to the convention by their progressive husbands—were not the most grievous victims of these injustices. Many of them were wealthy. Many of them were well educated. Most of them were white, blessed by the class and caste system of their time. They could have distracted themselves with plenty of other pursuits, been contented with their privileged lives. Instead, they were outraged about their rights and other people's rights too.

"Women do feel themselves aggrieved, oppressed and fraudulently deprived of their most sacred rights," the group wrote, and they would not rest until that changed. They were not naive, they did not expect this to merely happen. Rather, they had learned from Clarkson's campaign—one that they themselves had been involved in for years in the United States—and understood that there was a playbook by which rights could be won. "We shall employ agents, circulate tracts, petition the State and national Legislatures, and endeavor to enlist the pulpit and press in our behalf," they wrote, predicting convention after convention, wave after wave of resistance and pressure until all women got what they deserved.

Which happened to be exactly what it took.

After the Seneca Falls Convention in 1848, many waves followed, each one growing more diverse—economically and racially. In 1851, a woman named Sojourner Truth got up onstage and gave her famous "Ain't I a Woman?" speech. Although later accounts would present it in Southern slave dialect, Truth—a native of New York—spoke in perfect English. "I am a woman's rights," she said with complete confidence. "I have as much muscle as any man, and can do as much work as any man. I have plowed and reaped and husked and chopped and mowed, and can any man do more than that?"

She was triply discriminated against in her time. A woman. Black. A former slave. But there she was, demanding not only her seat at the table but fighting tirelessly for the postwar amendment, even though it effectively gave only black men their rights. But to her it wasn't about one group or one cause but about equality and dignity for all—however long that took. "I have been forty years a slave and forty years free," Sojourner Truth told an audience in 1867, "and would be here forty years more to have equal rights for all. I supposed I am kept here because something remains for me to do; I supposed I am yet to help break the chain."

What mattered now that the ice had been cracked, she said, was that they all kept stirring. That's what the Civil War was, that's what the Thirteenth, Fourteenth, and Fifteenth Amendments did.

Not content with that, in 1872 Susan B. Anthony, an abolitionist, feminist, and friend of Truth's, was ready to stir things up in a big way herself. "Well I have been & gone & done it!!" she told a friend, "positively voted the Republican ticket—strait—this A.M at 7Oclock & *swore my vote in at that.*" She was promptly arrested and put on trial. Defying the judge at sentencing, she refused to be silent or to comply. "I shall never pay a dollar of your unjust penalty," she said.

Freeing the slaves had required the violence of soldiers, but now women hoped to wage a different kind of war, against the state that enforced injustice. Where Susan B. Anthony was willing to defy a judge with words, the next generation of women went much further.

Across the Atlantic, Emmeline Pankhurst recalled her childhood memories of being taken to a fund-raiser for newly freed American slaves. After the death of her husband, she and her daughter would wage a ceaseless battle on behalf of women's rights. Unlike other suffrage associations, hers was built around two principles: First, that the right to vote was the cause from which all other women's issues could be addressed and thus their sole and exclusive focus. Second, that it was *deeds* and not *words* that mattered in that fight. "It is by going to prison, rather than by argument," Pankhurst would later explain, "that we have won the support of the English working man."

And they went to prison *a lot.*

For heckling politicians. For storming the stage at events. For the targeted destruction of public property—usually the throwing of stones at windows—to prove the point that society valued pretty much everything more than women. They were nonviolent, but that was a one-way street—the women came to wear cardboard under their dresses to protect themselves against the beatings they regularly got, while others trained in martial arts so that they could parry the blows of their much larger attackers.

Once in prison, they refused to comply further, undergoing hunger strikes to the point of near death. In a famous speech, which took its example from Cato, who died rather than serve Caesar, Pankhurst explained that she refused to accept the legitimacy of a government that so deprived its citizens. "You can kill that woman," she said of herself and her resisters, "but she escapes you then; you cannot govern her. No power on earth can govern a human being, however feeble, who withholds his or her consent." Indeed, one suffragette, Emily Davison, who had previously attempted a public suicide to protest the force feeding of the hunger-striking feminists in jail, was crushed by the king's horse in 1913 while holding a women's rights banner. Her gruesome death, intentional or not, captured by the news cameras, presaged the public martyrdom of Buddhist monk Thích Quảng Đức, who set himself on fire fifty years later. "One big tragedy," she had said earlier, "may save many others."

Meanwhile, back in America, women stood in front of the White House—Silent Sentinels, they were called—through the rain and sleet and grueling heat, as well as beatings and catcalls and arrests. Each one who was taken away was replaced by another, carrying picket signs that said "Mr. President. HOW LONG MUST WOMEN WAIT FOR LIBERTY?"

Carrie Chapman Catt, who was not even born until ten years after the Seneca Falls Convention, would later try to put into quantifiable terms how long this generational struggle took, just *what* it took:

To get the word "male" in effect out of the Constitution cost the women of the country fifty-two years of pauseless campaign . . . During that time they were forced to conduct fifty-six campaigns of referenda to male voters; 480 campaigns to get Legislatures to submit suffrage amendments to voters; 47 campaigns to get State constitutional conventions to write woman suffrage into state constitutions; 277

campaigns to get State party conventions to include woman suffrage planks; 30 campaigns to get presidential party conventions to adopt woman suffrage planks in party platforms, and 19 campaigns with 19 successive Congresses.

It was one woman after another, one convention after another, one campaign after another, each offering its own small measure of devotion.

They would not be deterred. They would not be divided.

Certainly, there were attempts to divide them. Southern women were criticized for associating with black women. Northern women with lower-class women. Eastern women for opening their tent to western Mormon women. And while many of the women involved in the women's rights movement had blind spots, even abhorrent views about class or race, they managed to put together a shockingly broad coalition.

"For the first time in the woman movement," Carrie Chapman Catt would say at the opening of the seventh conference of the International Woman Suffrage Alliance in Budapest in 1913, "it is expected that Hindu, Buddhist, Confucian, Mohammedan, Jewish and Christian women will sit together in a Congress uniting their voices in a common plea for the liberation of their sex from those artificial discriminations which every political and religious system has directed against them."

In fact, the movement had been broad and diverse from the

beginning. Thomas Wentworth Higginson, a prominent Bostonian who translated Epictetus and later led black troops in the Civil War, had long called for a national convention for women's rights. Frederick Douglass, then just thirty years old, actually attended Seneca Falls. "There are few facts in my humble history," he said at the end of his life, "to which I look back with more satisfaction, than . . . that I was sufficiently enlightened at that early day, and then only a few years from slavery, to support [the] resolution for woman suffrage."

Why would this man, himself in constant danger of being kidnapped and sold back into slavery at any moment, take the time to fight for *someone else's rights*?

Because, as the poet Frances Ellen Watkins Harper would explain in a New York church immediately following the Civil War, justice was not fulfilled if *anyone* was unequal before the law. "We are all bound together," she said, "in one great bundle of humanity." Our fates are tied up with each other's, she understood, and the sooner people realize that, the better we'll all be, the more we'll all be able to do.

As abolitionism led to the fight for women's rights—one torch lighting another—the fight for women's rights led to civil rights. It was another long fight, but it accomplished so much as it went. As women earned their right to vote, state by state, child labor laws were passed. The stranglehold that political bosses had on American cities began to loosen. The first welfare laws were brought into being. So were the first protests against genocide, in this case led by Alice Stone Blackwell, who thought that her feminist work was inseparable from her work supporting refugees from the Armenian genocide. "Men are saying perhaps, 'Thank God, this everlasting woman's right is over!'" Crystal Eastman, a feminist and suffragette, would say after the passage of the Nineteenth Amendment, "but women, if I know them, are saying, 'Now at last we can begin.'"

Eastman herself would prove that, going on to found the ACLU. In 1955, Rosa Parks, trained in self-discipline and nonviolence and activism by the NAACP and the Highlander Folk School, refused to get up from her seat on a bus.* An ad hoc boycott followed. At a church in Montgomery, E. D. Nixon got up to urge that it continue, that this was the place to stand and fight. "You preachers been eating these women's fried chicken long enough without doing anything for them," he said. Were they going to do their duty? Were they going to stand up for Rosa Parks? Or was he to tell his parishioners that they were too afraid? "I am not a coward!" a twenty-six-year-old Martin Luther King Jr. replied.

What followed then was a movement that borrowed on all the lessons learned by Clarkson, by the suffragettes, by Jesus, by

---

* It's worth noting that Rosa Parks was not actually the first black woman to stage a protest on public transportation. A young girl named Claudette Colvin tried it nine months earlier and Sojourner Truth did it nearly a hundred years before both in Washington, D.C.

Gandhi, by Thoreau. King himself would pick up and claim as his own that line from Frances Ellen Watkins Harper, that we were tied up in a bundle of humanity.

Freedom, he said, has a "'we' quality"—wanting it, striving for it, fighting for it helps not just yourself but *everyone* else.

He wasn't just fighting for his own rights or Rosa Parks's rights but for the very soul of the nation, to demand that it live out the meaning of its creed and faith. Once again, this was a multigenerational, multidenominational, multiracial fight. King himself had first been spurred by Parks, and he would be spurred again by the leadership of Diane Nash and a group of college students who gathered in Nashville for the first sit-ins of the civil rights movement. Together, they would bring with them elderly people, white people, rich people, poor people, Jews, Muslims, Southern people, Northern people, people from all over the world.

Many of those people had been previously content with how things were, quite convinced this was not their fight. One woman, Mary Peabody, was as blue-blooded as an American could be—the wife of retired bishop Malcolm Peabody of the Episcopal Church of Central New York. Recruited by activists savvy enough to understand that the arrest of Northern whites would make for bigger news, Mary agreed to go down to St. Augustine where the movement was on campaign, quite confident it was all a big misunderstanding. "I do not believe they will deny me the pleasure of lunch with my Negro friend," she said as she left.

Almost immediately, this grandmother of seven was denied communion at a local church because she had been branded a "radical" by the congregation. Then, while attempting that lunch with her friend, they were told to go eat outside. Hoping to appeal to better angels, the friends tried again at a small motor lodge down the street, only to be forcefully confronted by an armed sheriff and a pack of German shepherds.

Ms. Peabody was nobody's idea of a radical before, but she was one now. "I think I better call my son," she told her hosts, and with that she called *Governor* Endicott Peabody of Massachusetts to let him know that in a few minutes his seventy-two-year-old mother was going to be arrested in Florida for defying an unjust law.

"You look just like Miss Eleanor Roosevelt," one of the black activists said to her as the guards walked her down the hall of the jail in a conservative pink dress suit. "We are cousins," Mary Peabody said with a twinkle. Although two hundred other people were arrested, her picture made the front page of newspapers across the country, the *New York Times* showing this smiling Northern church lady behind bars, the officer behind her armed with a *cattle prod* as if he might have to use it.

Peabody would spend the next two days in jail, preferring to stay with her new friends rather than be bailed out. "After I arrived, I began to see things differently," she explained. So did activists and ordinary citizens alike.

"I have been so deeply inspired by your mother's creative witness in Florida," Martin Luther King Jr. would write in a telegram to the governor of Massachusetts. "Through her words and action she is saying to the whole nation that all men are brothers and that the cancerous sore of segregation must be removed from the body politic before our democratic health will be realized."

Once again, change happens when people get outraged about other people's rights.

Wedgwood's logo had asked, "Am I Not a Man and a Brother?" Now the protestors did not ask, they made the statement: "I am a Man." More, they *showed* they were human beings—human beings capable of dignity and grace and incredible courage. Of course, they had always been these things, but through the medium of television and expertly chosen showdowns, through that creative witness, they forced the world to see it.

Everything was planned, practiced, a result of exacting discipline. "If a person was taking a severe beating," Diane Nash explained, "we would practice other people putting their bodies in between that person and the violence. . . . We would practice not striking back, if someone struck us." In confrontation after confrontation, the authority of the police and the political power structure was diminished. The strength, the moral righteousness of the protestors was made unassailable, even as—no, *because*—the blows landed on their exposed bodies.

"The sheriff is not after you," one civil rights strategist explained, "you are after the sheriff." They were relentless. They wanted to go to jail. They were not afraid of being hurt or dying. They were pressing, pushing, they would not be deterred. "You can turn your back on me," the Reverend C. T. Vivian told one racist police leader, "but you can't turn your back on justice." He was pushed down a flight of stairs in response—a cowardly, violent act caught perfectly by a news camera. "What kind of people are you?" Vivian shouted back, words destined to be repeated in a thousand news articles. "What do you tell your children at night? What do you tell your wives at night?"

After X-rays and a checkup from the doctor, Vivian marched again the next day.

"One of the things that I have learned over the years," Diane Nash said, "is that you really can't change anyone but yourself and what we did in the South was change ourselves from people who could be segregated into people who could no longer be segregated. The attitude became 'well kill us if that's what you're going to do, but you cannot segregate us any longer' and once you change yourself the world has to fit up against the new you."

No matter what happened, how bleak or dark it got, they kept their eye on the prize.

What prize?

Freedom.

Justice.

Love.

Just as it is impossible to truly ascertain the *first* step in the march of justice, it is also—thankfully—impossible to claim it has ended. Martin Luther King Jr. would spend the last years of his short life committed to the antiwar movement. A year after his death, there was the uprising at Stonewall. In this same moment, Ralph Nader, long before his fame as a third-party political candidate, assembled a small group of lawyers—dubbed Nader's Raiders—who would begin the ongoing fight to protect the public against the abuses of corporate interests.

Animal rights. Environmental rights. Voting rights. Gay rights. Consumer rights. Reproductive rights. Antipoverty activists. Anticolonial activists. Peace activists. Prison reformers. Fighters of human trafficking. Free speech advocates.

Wave after wave, generation after generation. Seeking a more perfect union, realizing the true promise of the social contract.

Justice is not a thing that happens, it's something that is made, that is continuing to be made, even as you read this.

By people who get together, by people who care.

Sometimes because it affects them directly. Often and most beautifully when it does not.

People who want to leave the world better than they found it. People who see something and say something. People who make friends . . . and good trouble. People who are patient . . . but at the same time refuse to delay. People with a north star . . . bigger than themselves, bigger than their own interests. People with big plans . . . but start small, start with what they can do right now. People who don't just stand there, who refuse to be neutral, who accept their responsibility. People who get things done. People who not only do their jobs but do them generously, selflessly.

Ordinary people . . . who become extraordinary.

"Those men and women are fortunate," Emmeline Pankhurst would write in her memoir, "who are born at a time when a great struggle for human freedom is in progress. It is an added good fortune to have parents who take a personal part in the movements of their time."

Well, that time is now. All the misfortunes of the world, all that is happening around us—it's both an obstacle and an opportunity. It's a chance for us to struggle . . . to be part of the struggle. If our parents didn't do enough, so be it. We can make up for that. We can be the example that our children, that the people who come after us look back at.

Justice is a kind of endless passing of torches, an unfinished march that started long ago that each generation joins and continues in its own way.

Or doesn't.

Such is the power of each and every one of us in the moment we happen to be born.

We have the power . . .

. . . to care

. . . to help others

. . . to learn how to create change

. . . to be generous

. . . to build bonds

. . . to stand up for the little guy.

But it's not a question of power, it's a question of will.

Will you?

You Just Have to Be Kind

⁓

How did Emperor Hadrian know? How did he know that Antoninus—whom he had no blood relation to—could be trusted with the throne? It seems like an incredible leap.

A man with absolute power giving that absolute power to another man with only a promise to go on that he would protect and guide young Marcus Aurelius—the truest one—to one day rule in his place.

But to Hadrian it wasn't a leap, because he felt that he had glimpsed into Antoninus's character. It was a minor moment but a revealing one. He had watched Antoninus, who had no idea anyone was looking, carefully, respectfully guide his ailing father-in-law up the stairs.

A simple act of kindness, given freely and casually to an old man in need, was the decisive vote. It told Hadrian what he needed to know.

History is replete with brilliant and successful men and women. You've probably encountered plenty in your life. But how many truly kind people have you met? Why else is it shocking when you come across someone doing something genuinely nice for someone else?

We're not asking much of people . . . but it's so rare. "Welcome to Earth, young man," the novelist Kurt Vonnegut once wrote to a fan. "It's hot in the summer and cold in the winter. At the outside you've got a hundred years here. There's only one rule that I know of: Goddamn it, Joe, you've got to be kind."*

Kind to strangers.

Kind to people who you work with or work for you.

Kind to someone who just made a mistake.

Kind to both customers and vendors.

Kind to someone you dislike.

Kind to the future, to generations not yet born.

When we look back at history, one thing that never ages well is a lack of kindness. The mobs yelling at little black children going to school for the first time. The way colonizers treated the people there before them. The role women were relegated to in society for so long. Sure, legally, these were seriously unjust situations. But before that, perhaps partly explaining how such injustices came to pass, there was some profound failure of em-

---

*J. M. Barrie, the creator of Peter Pan, would articulate the same rule in 1902: "Shall we make a new rule of life from tonight: Always try to be a little kinder than is necessary?"

pathy, of kindness. It was the inability to conceive of the other as a person as someone deserving of decency.

That's the golden rule, right? Treat others how you would want to be treated. And who wants to be treated any way other than kindly? With respect? With fairness?

It's not just a rule, it's a way of living. The Stoics said we should try to see every person we meet as *an opportunity for kindness*. This is a wonderful change in perspective. It transforms daily life, as challenging and noxious as it can be, into a series of changes, one after another, to be nice, to do something nice, to be considerate, to make a positive difference.

It doesn't matter that we're tired. That we're busy. That we were ourselves just treated with unkindness.

Respond with kindness. Err on the side of compassion. Do the helpful thing.

In the early days of the Blitz, Clementine Churchill had to write a note to her husband to remind him of this very fact. "My Darling Winston," she wrote, "I must confess that I have noticed a deterioration in your manner; & you are not so kind as you used to be." Yes, he had power, she noted, but it was precisely this power over people—the ability to fire anyone and everyone at whim—that obligated him to be polite and kind and, most of all, calm, even when he was upset. "You won't get the best results by irascibility & rudeness," she reminded him. "They will breed either dislike or a slave mentality."

Admiral Rickover was notoriously brusque. He was a yeller

too. But the people who worked for him understood that he cared—not just for the work and about safety but them personally. That's essential, and it's better than the opposite masked with politeness. Still, there is not a person or team (or a child) alive that would not appreciate a nice word on top . . . and they cost us so little.

There is no leader ever who has not had to deal with frustrations. There is no smart person who has not had to suffer fools. There is no good person who has not been ill-treated or had enemies. This is just how it goes.

But it is our authority, our intelligence, our decency that obligates us to be kind despite all this. As Vonnegut said, it's the only goddamn rule there is.

It doesn't always have to be some big thing.

What about a smile? What about noticing a job well done? The holding open of a door? A favor rendered? The choice to invite, to pick up the tab for lunch, to compliment, to encourage, to volunteer, to hand your box of leftovers to the man begging on the street corner, or give your spouse a bouquet of flowers?

You never know what low moment you might be rescuing a person from. You never know how they'll pay this forward. But in a sense, it doesn't matter—at least that's not why we do it.

We do it because it's the discipline we practice. We do it because being kind is the more courageous thing in a cynical world. We do it because it's right—because people *deserve* kindness and because kindness *makes us better.*

At the end of his life, as he lay dying, Marcus Aurelius had one regret, one thing he was still chastising himself for. The times he had lost his temper, the times he had been unkind.

And when we survey our lives, we will think the same thing. We'll forget all our reasons. We'll forget all the causes. We'll forget what had been done to us. All we'll wish is that we'd been a little nicer, a little less clever, and a lot more kind.

Well?

Well, it's not too late.

See How the Other Half Lives

~

Beatrice Webb grew up in a well-to-do British family. Unlike many women in her time, she was allowed an education at the best schools. Not that she needed to think about getting a job or supporting herself. Soon enough she was courted by rich and handsome men, and quite nearly married a future prime minister.

It was only under the guise of a sociological project, stemming from the Charity Organisation Society, that Beatrice, after two and a half decades on this planet, got what she would call her "first chance of personal intimacy, on terms of social equality, with a wage-earning family."

Pretending to be a simple farmer's daughter named Miss Jones, she went to live with distant relatives to experience and study their world. It was just a few miles from her home, but it may as well have been on another planet.

It wasn't simply that Webb was young and sheltered. In fact, society at that time was *designed* to shelter, keeping the upper classes safely ensconced from the grinding poverty of the vast majority of the population and the injustices that caused it . . . and the lower classes kept apart so they could not become equals with their "betters."

There were then, in Britain and indeed in every developed country, Benjamin Disraeli would explain, "Two nations; between whom there is no intercourse and no sympathy; who are as ignorant of each other's habits, thoughts, and feelings, as if they were dwellers in different zones, or inhabitants of different planets; who are formed by a different breeding, are fed by a different food, are ordered by different manners, and are not governed by the same laws . . . THE RICH AND THE POOR."

Webb's experiment shattered all these artificial barriers, changing not only her perspective but the future of social organization. There in the factories and shipyards and slums, she saw how the other half lived. She had previously been a believer in "laissez-faire" economics, a belief that did not survive contact with the humanity whom it cast aside. The model of charity at that time—which assumed that the poor were immoral and needed to be reformed—was revealed as woefully insufficient and cruel.

What would emerge from this eye-opening experience was Beatrice's lifelong work as a social activist. Among her long list of accomplishments, Beatrice first coined the concept of "collective bargaining," founded the London School of Economics, relaunched the Labour Party, and helped form the Fabian Society, which today we would call a progressive think tank. She fought for a social safety net in Britain, fought against poverty and exploitation wherever she found it.

Most social change is a result of a similar kind of rude awakening. Someone sees something and decides to do something.

In 1882, a twenty-four-year-old state senator named Theodore Roosevelt found himself as the potentially decisive vote in a bill pushed for by the Cigar-Makers' Union that aimed to improve working conditions for thousands of poor workers who labored in the city's tenements. Roosevelt was initially opposed to it, like Beatrice Webb, believing it was "contrary to the principles of political economy of the *laissez-faire* kind." But Roosevelt was far from laissez-faire in how he formed his opinions, so he actually went and visited these slums for himself, hardly believing the accounts he had received from Samuel Gompers, the labor organizer behind the bill.

This slum was how many blocks from where he grew up? Yet he'd never been there. But what he saw changed him forever. Forty years later, Roosevelt would still speak of it with horror. Considering the explanations that Roosevelt would later make about how he was not "a sentimentalist," we can safely assume he broke down in tears as he watched emaciated children sleeping six or seven to a bed, as he watched families struggle to breathe among all the chemicals, as the stench and filth overwhelmed his senses.

"What are you going to do about it," the activist Jacob Riis would write in his famous book *How the Other Half Lives*, "is the main question of the day." After he learned, the answer for Roosevelt was simple: "I've come to help," he told Riis, who became a lifelong friend. Indeed, for the rest of his life, Roosevelt would fight on behalf of the exploited and against entrenched and powerful interests.

The same thing happened to Lyndon B. Johnson. Johnson's childhood was the opposite of Roosevelt's. His parents were born in a log cabin. He knew poverty and struggle and deprivation firsthand. But he was, as a white man in the American caste system, still higher than any of the other lower classes. Two experiences showed him something he could not *un*-see.

First, it was teaching at a school for the children of Mexican American farmers in the town of Cotulla, Texas, where the people were treated, as Johnson put it, "just worse than you'd treat a dog." He'd never forget the scene watching the "Mexican children going through a garbage pile, shaking the coffee grounds from the grapefruit rinds and sucking the rinds for the juice that was left."

Second, after decades of indifference to the pains of segregation, it was the experiences of his black housekeeper and cook, Zephyr Wright, that finally broke him of his obliviousness to a racist world. When Johnson asked Zephyr to drive the family dog from Washington back to the Johnson ranch in Texas, she begged him not to send her. *It's hard enough for a black person to drive across the South without a dog,* Zephyr explained. "When we drive to Texas and I have to go to the restroom like Bird or the girls, I'm not allowed to go to the bathroom. I have to find a bush and squat. When it comes time to eat, we can't go into restaurants. We have to eat out of a brown bag. And at night [my husband] sleeps in the front of the car with the steering wheel around his neck and I sleep in the back." Johnson left the conversation in tears and powerfully relayed these experiences to other lawmakers, who helped him champion the Civil Rights Act of 1964.

The problem is that it's so easy to stay in our bubbles. To not see what we don't want to see. We don't do the math—on what it would be like to live on such a wage, on where all these raw materials are coming from, on where our money is going. We ignore the smell . . . or let people cover it up for us. (There's a joke that the Royal Family *thinks the world smells like fresh paint.*)

But even those of us who are struggling, who have their own problems, can be guilty of the same sin. When you're suffering in your own life, it's hard to muster the empathy to see someone else's—especially if you or your choices have played any part in it.

As a kind of converse to the idea that we shouldn't go around with people who make us blush, we should actively seek out learning things that make us blush. We need to learn about the unpleasant facts of history. We need to learn about the inequities of society. We need to become vacuums for the lived experiences of other people—what makes it hard to be them, where they struggle, where they have been mistreated, where their daily lives are different than ours.

The truth is that injustices are everywhere. Transparency is, as we know, not a widely practiced virtue.

Unpleasantness is swept from view. Disparities and their consequences are covered up. The sufferings and desperate needs of millions are kept from us . . . and we keep ourselves from them.

Steve Jobs apparently never visited any of Apple's factories in China. He was a designer, not a manufacturer, more interested in his gadgets than the conditions in which they were made.

But this is not an excuse, as Riis said, it is an indictment.

Did you not know? Or did you just not *care* to know?

We cannot fix what we won't face. We cannot stop what we refuse to acknowledge.*

We must wake up. We must seek out the experiences that will change us, we must seek out an understanding of how the world works and lives. We can't wait for someone to show us. We can't assume we know. We can't accept appearances.

The epiphanies of Webb and Roosevelt and Johnson were not free or fun. They were massively disruptive, not just in the

---

* But what of the people who do find out and still don't care? We should pity these folks too—something is broken in them.

sense that the experiences shook their worldview but also in that it redirected the course of their lives.

It was not possible for decent people to continue as they always had.

The knowledge demanded action.

So go forth and find.

You Have to Help

J oseph P. Kennedy, the father of future president John F. Kennedy, was the U.S. ambassador to the United Kingdom from 1938 to 1940.

Germany rushed to rearm, portending not just war but the Holocaust, which was the logical—in fact, promised—end of Hitler's vision. Famine. Destruction. Carnage. The signs were all there . . . so too were the opportunities to prevent it.

Instead, Kennedy, an isolationist, urged restraint. He made false equivalences and raised "whataboutisms." He blamed the victims. He tried to meet with Hitler. He supported appeasement. He discouraged any potential American aid to Britain, even as the bombs fell. It wasn't that bad, he said at first, then later that it was hopeless.

Joseph P. Kennedy was not some secret Nazi, but like a lot of people then and now, he wanted a looming problem to not be his problem. He was looking for a way not to have to care. To not have to get involved. To not have to risk anything.

So perhaps we should forgive his son John for misquoting

Edmund Burke when speaking to the Canadian Parliament as president in 1961. "The only thing necessary for the triumph of evil," Kennedy had said in quotation, "is for good men to do nothing." Burke had said no such thing, but the gist of the idea had rung true for a son haunted by his father's cowardice and cruelty, and the loss of his brother in the war that his dad had helped allow to happen.*

Even Kennedy's foreign policy overreaches—in Vietnam and in the Bay of Pigs—take on a different light with this context. So too does his steel-spined response to the Cuban Missile Crisis. Kennedy learned, by terrible experience, that there is no such thing as neutrality in a world where evil exists. He learned that cancer, if ignored, metastasizes. And this also explains another misquotation Kennedy frequently made: "Dante once said that the hottest places in hell are reserved for those who in a period of moral crisis maintain their neutrality."

The quotes weren't factual . . . but considering his father, they were Freudian.

They are also illustrative for the issues of today. Because the thing about letting evil triumph is that it's not just wrong, it's usually stupid and self-defeating too.

---

* Kennedy's college thesis was titled "Appeasement at Munich," which was turned into a book titled *Why England Slept*. With almost no self-awareness, his father funded an effort to turn it into a bestseller to advance his son's political career.

In the fall of 1985, almost no one knew what crack cocaine was. Within a year, it was consuming American cities like a wildfire. Hospitals filled up. Crime spiked. The foster care system was deluged. Guns flooded the streets and the murder rate doubled. The media covered every grotesque and terrible moment in real time, stoking the flames of the secondary moral panic that followed.

Yet as far as solutions went, most of the United States shrugged. The "crack epidemic" did not affect them. And even though the nation's inner cities were the direct legacy of slavery and Jim Crow, they absolved themselves of responsibility. It was an "urban issue," a cultural problem. It was the victims' own fault.

More than just unfair and cruel, a once-in-a-lifetime opportunity was lost, as they'd soon see.

Because in the late 1990s, just as the crack cocaine epidemic waned, a new drug epidemic began to prey on Americans. This time it wasn't primarily black Americans in inner cities who were the victims, but also white Americans and affluent Americans and rural Americans, indeed *every* kind of American was vulnerable to it. It would be a far bigger wildfire than the last time—an industrialized, corporate, and medically driven one—and its death toll far larger.

Where were the treatment centers? Where were the prevention policies? Where were the investments to keep people from falling behind? Where were the agencies that could bring people together to tackle this problem? In the moment that millions of people most needed it, they weren't there. Because nobody had cared enough to start building them fifteen years earlier.*

It was, as indifference to suffering so often is, a kind of illustration of Martin Niemöller's famous poem "First they came..."

You know the one.

First they came for the socialists, and I did not speak out—
Because I was not a socialist.
Then they came for the trade unionists,
    and I did not speak out—
Because I was not a trade unionist.
Then they came for the Jews, and I did not speak out—
Because I was not a Jew.
Then they came for me—and there was no one left
    to speak for me.

When you shrug at the suffering of someone else, you invite it, inevitably, on yourself and people you love down the line.

---

*COVID-19 was a similar parable. How much safer would everyone have been in a society with a better safety net and a better health-care system? How many variants might have been prevented with a faster, cheaper global vaccination effort?

Martin Niemöller would write his famous poem after he found himself, a Christian, in Dachau, where he nearly died. Someone later asked how he could have been so self-absorbed, so silent when it mattered. "I am paying for that mistake now," he said, "and not me alone, but thousands of other persons like me."

It's a very natural human impulse to not get involved. It's almost by definition the *easier* option. There is even a way that virtue can justify it: *I'm just minding my own business. I've got my own troubles. I don't want to make things worse. I don't know if I am qualified. It's a complicated situation. It's really expensive. I'll just wait and see.*

In the light of an impossible, complicated, overwhelming problem, we send our "thoughts and prayers" instead. We try to sit on "two stools" as Cicero did, waiting for divisive issues to sort themselves out. We betray ourselves and them in the process.

But eventually, the paucity of all these excuses falls apart. We're left with the stark horrors of what's happening, we come face-to-face with our basic human obligation to help the helpless, to do what we can to prevent suffering.

That's what happened to Truman. His childhood had been a lie—that's what Southern culture was built around, the very structure of society oppressed and tortured their black neighbors. But as Truman saw more of the world, the scales fell from his eyes. "I can't approve of such goings on and I shall never approve it, as long as I am here," he wrote patiently to one particularly bigoted friend in 1948 after another lynching.* This was an important sentiment but far less important than the words that came after it: "I am going to try to remedy it."

That's what responsibility is, Rickover said, that which forces man to become *involved*. To try to help. To try to solve.

Not that every problem is going to be standing up to the Nazis or the Soviets, or rushing in to call the paramedics for Kitty Genovese while your neighbors turn up their televisions. It could be as simple as attending a PTA meeting or voting. It's the decision to do more than complain, more than blame. It's the decision to participate.

Because our disengagement necessitates the engagement of someone else. Or worse, it means the empowerment of someone or something else—something not good, not honest, not kind, not accountable or transparent.

"Silence in the face of evil is itself evil," Dietrich Bonhoeffer said from inside Hitler's Germany. "God will not hold us guiltless. Not to speak is to speak. Not to act is to act." Remember that you can commit injustice by doing nothing also, Marcus Aurelius wrote to himself in *Meditations*.

---

*When one Southern supporter asked him for reassurance that he wouldn't shove "miscegenation" down their throats, Truman whipped out a copy of the Bill of Rights from his pocket and read it to them. "I'm everybody's president," he said.

Those are real quotes. Will the truth of them haunt your legacy?

History tells us what happens when people let evil act with impunity, when suffering is ignored or allowed to happen. It doesn't work out well . . . including for the people who turned away or dallied when they could have made a difference.

We may not succeed, especially right away. But each time someone stoops to help someone in need, each time a society involves itself in a problem that affects just a few of its members, they're not just strengthening the muscles of the heart but building new muscles too. These muscles, this experience, these tools developed, these lessons learned from one crisis become assets and equity that will someday be of use to you or someone you know.

You are also sending a message, not just to the people you are helping—that they matter, that you care—but to everyone else. You are showing who you stand with. You are demonstrating what justice looks like.

By tackling civil rights, America not only addressed a profound injustice . . . it also got a better political system. It got better politicians. By fighting back against the forces that enforced segregation, Americans weren't just protecting minorities, they were strengthening their own rights to free speech, to vote, to fair trials, against police intimidation and mistreatment, against mob violence. This also gave the country a stronger claim to the moral high ground in the Cold War against totalitarianism abroad.

By helping others, you help yourself—not just because we're all part of that garment of mutuality, but because a government and society that knows how to help one group is going to be less likely to fall catastrophically when it has to help a different group—or a lot of groups.

By indifference, you also commit self-harm . . . but by the time you realize it, it will be too late.

Start Small

~

The liberation and empowerment of women was a complete transformation of society. But its first legal manifestations were quite small and almost forgettably technical.

In the 1860s, John Stuart Mill, then a member of Parliament who had been convinced of women's rights by his strong and brilliant wife, Harriet Taylor Mill, added an amendment to a voting bill that sought to change the wording of the bill from "man" to "person," a tiny tweak in language with potentially enormous legal implications. Some laughed, some were outraged at its timidity—but all parties missed the revolution that had quietly begun.*

As they say, we have to start *somewhere.*

But the problem is that if we are too ambitious, too lofty—

---

* It's worth noting here in this footnote how important footnotes have been in legal decisions over the years—they are not binding by law but have often planted the seeds from which future (and transformative) legal decisions are made.

or some would say, too naive—we may not get *anywhere*. Mother Teresa would see this quite clearly, not just as her calling but as a practical and realistic place to start. "If I look at the mass," she said, "I will never act. If I look at the one, I will."

We can despair of the whole, we can tilt at the windmills of enormous problems, we can talk endlessly of utopian futures . . . or we can get to work.

On the person in front of us. On the thing in front of us. Reeling from a personal crisis and a sense of despair about the world, a woman wrote to the psychologist Carl Jung. His advice was to "quietly do the next and most necessary thing," that if she took the smallest, most viable step in front of her, she would always be making progress, always be doing something meaningful.

It's small but it is not nothing. In fact, it's everything.

There is an old story about a boy who comes upon a beach that is covered in starfish, hundreds, thousands of them washed up on the shore. It's an appalling, tragic sight, and on the verge of tears, he begins to throw them, one by one, back into the sea.

"It doesn't matter," an adult tells him. "You'll never even make a dent in this."

"It matters to this starfish," the boy says, as he rescues another one.

To the person you're saving, to the person whose burden you are lessening? There is nothing "small" about it. When the Talmud says that he who saves one person saves the world, maybe that's partly what they meant—because you certainly save *that person's whole world.*

Despite the expression "all politics are local," we tend to think big picture before we think little picture. We think grand gestures, complete solutions instead of progress, instead of doing something for the people or suffering in front of us.

But no change is possible without that first, tiny step.

Think of Thomas Clarkson. His essay had been about the moral question of whether it was right or wrong to own a person against their will. Although he came to believe the answer was *no,* that's not where his activism started—he focused first only on ending the slave *trade.* In fact, not even the global slave trade, but only *within the British Empire.* Think of Truman. When he decided to get involved in civil rights, there wasn't much he could do. He started by appointing a commission. He followed that with an executive order to desegregate the armed forces, an executive order to desegregate the federal government alongside it.

It wasn't enough, but it was a start.

But in doing that, in making the first motion, you are making a powerful statement—perhaps the most powerful statement in the whole speech. You are saying hope is not dead. Decency is not dead. You are carrying the fire, you are keeping the light alive.

We begin with ourselves, our own standards, the things we immediately control. How we run our lives, our business, how we do our work. Next, we focus on what is closest to us, with the good we can do in front of us, the first bit of progress we can make. Make one person happier. Help make one thing better.

This is small but it is no small thing. In fact, if we all do that, the world *is* changed.

This world is filled with overwhelming, intractable issues. We face massive "collective action problems," as they're called. And yet it falls to each of us to do what we can, where we can, with what we have.

As it was written in the Daodejing:

The difficult undertakings in the world all start with what is easy.

The great undertakings in the world all begin with what is small.

Picking up trash that we come across. Helping a friend get back on their feet. Raising good kids. Boycotting tea that's contributing to the slave trade, as countless activists did in the eighteenth and nineteenth centuries. "Say not that small's the sphere in which we move," the abolitionist poet Mary Birkett Card wrote of all the women who couldn't vote but could make a difference through their consumer habits.

But also voting—yes, voting. Because it makes a difference. "Every member of Dexter must be a registered voter," Martin

Luther King Jr. declared in his church in 1954. This wasn't as transformational a declaration as his "Dream," but it was a start. It was also an urgent opportunity, given that less than 5 percent of blacks in Alabama had registered at that point. And beginning somewhere? That was what counted. One of his few mistakes as a leader came during the Albany campaign, which fizzled out. "The mistake I made there," King explained, "was to protest against segregation generally rather than against a single and distinct facet of it."

Because honestly, we have no idea where things will end up, where this thing we started will take us. Lincoln, like Clarkson, started incrementally, even pragmatically. He did not initially set out to free the slaves or remake America along the principles the founders had set out but failed to live up to. He was not sure that was even possible. Instead, he began his political career with something much smaller—all he hoped to do was stop the *expansion* of slavery into new territories.

Thoreau himself argued that slavery would fall when *one* person opted out of the system. It matters not, he said, "how small a beginning may seem to be." Besides, if we don't begin, not only are we depriving the future of what could have been, but we are also *complicit* in what's happening here in the present.

Each of us is capable of taking a step. Each of us can do a little good . . . and this little good adds up. Like the folk protest song goes, we can be the *drops of water falling on the stone,* or like the story popular with sports teams, we can each pound the rock, and eventually, inevitably, one of those hammer blows will finally crack it.

As one civil rights marcher said when they were asked if the movement would win: "We won when we started."

That's right.

Let us begin.

Create Alliances

Harvey Milk, one of the first openly gay politicians in America, succeeded because he had allies. Not "allies" in the modern, progressive sense of the word—supporters of the LGBTQ community—but political allies. The kind you horse-trade with. The kind that Milk had himself cultivated, despite the fact that they were very different from him, and in fact didn't agree with his lifestyle at all.

It began in 1973, when the Teamsters Union was on strike against a number of beer distributors over a new union contract. The Teamsters needed the support of gay bars in San Francisco to put pressure on the beer companies. Harvey was willing to help . . . provided that the union began allowing gay drivers into the union.

"If we in the gay community want others to help us in our fight to end discrimination," Harvey Milk would later write, "then we must help others in their fights." So the gays and the Teamsters teamed up, quite successfully, in fact, culminating in a highly publicized boycott of Coors over a pretty standard labor contract.

And then when it came time for Harvey to run for San Francisco's board of supervisors, he had favors to call in.

"Whaddaya mean you're thinkin' of endorsin' this Harvey Milk guy?" the head of the mechanics union said when he heard the ask. "For Chrissakes, I'm supposed to go back to work and tell the guys we endorsed some goddamn fruit for a supervisor?" But Harvey's Teamster friends had an answer: "Hey. Harvey Milk's the guy who's been getting Coors beer out of gay bars." And so it went, among the candidates, Harvey was the closest thing the unions had to an ally, and so they in turn allied with him. "I know the guy's a fruit, but he shoots straight with us," said the city's union boss, George Evankovich. "Let's support him."

And they did, in election after election, until eventually he won, finally putting to use a pen and pencil set that his first Teamster friend had given him after he'd been wowed by Harvey's ability to organize. "You'll need it once you get to City Hall to sign bills," the man had said.

Indeed, Harvey did.

Look, it would be wonderful if causes succeeded because they were right. It would be wonderful if pioneers and barrier-breakers were supported because people cared about fairness and representation. But they don't and that's not how the system—or history—works.

As a kid, Harry Truman made a friend named Eddie Jacobson. America then was not just racist but also virulently antisemitic, and Jacobson was one of the few Jewish people Truman had ever met. They became closer during their stint in the army together, and afterward it was Jacobson whom Truman started—and failed—in the clothing business with.

It was a direct result of his conversations with his friend that Truman spoke publicly in 1943 about the horrors of the persecutions of the Jews in Europe, long before the true horrors of the Holocaust were widely known, warning that "merely talking about the Four Freedoms is not enough. This is the time for action." It was not a Jewish problem, he said, but an American one that needed to be faced "squarely and honorably." But then again, that's exactly who Truman was: a man loyal to his friends. A man who, like all of us, is shaped by the people we meet and the things we experience firsthand.

In 1948, though, Truman was at odds with Jewish leaders. His political advisors believed that Israel would be bad for foreign oil interests. Truman himself was put off by the number of diplomats who had come to forcefully make their case to him, going as far as to ban the mention of it in his office. No one could get a meeting with him on the topic. No one could change his mind.

Except Eddie Jacobson, who dropped by the White House without an appointment on a Saturday morning. Within minutes he was ushered in to speak to the president, after being warned at the door not to bring up Israel.

But that was precisely why he was there.

"Mr. President," Jacobson said, wondering if perhaps his friend still harbored some of the prejudices of his upbringing. "I haven't said a word, but every time I think of the homeless Jews, homeless for thousands of years . . . I start crying." Then, actually crying, Jacobson made an appeal that only a longtime ally, that only a true friend could make. "Now you refuse to see [Dr. Chaim Weizmann, one of Israel's chief advocates] because you were insulted by some of our American Jewish leaders," he said to Truman. "It doesn't sound like you, Harry."

It was the last line that seemed to hit Truman the hardest. He paused for a very long time and then turned his chair. "You win, you bald-headed son of a bitch."

Exactly two months later, just eleven minutes after Israel proclaimed its existence, America would be the first country to recognize the Jewish homeland.

Israel's journey was a long one, born of many sacrifices—sacrifices that continue to this day—nor was it a perfect geopolitical solution, which is why consequences from that decision continue to this day as well. But the fact is that Israel almost certainly would not exist without Jacobson's intervention. "Don't forget for a single moment that Harry S. Truman is the most powerful single man in the world," Weizmann had told Jacobson. "You have a job to do; so keep the White House doors open."

Justice, you might say, is a team sport. Very few of us are able to do much alone. So why do so many people choose to do precisely that? Purity? Ego? Ignorance?

What it's not done out of is a desire to get things done.

Our model should be Thomas Clarkson, bringing together three Anglicans and nine Quakers at that print shop meeting. As the antislavery movement grew, he was constantly adding new allies, new voices, diverse voices, working with everyone he could to advance his cause. That's what the suffragettes did too—it was a big tent of women of different faiths, different backgrounds, different political persuasions. Some swore off marriage, while others, like the Mormon suffragettes at the time, were polygamous. Some thought women deserved complete equality, others just the right to vote. But they were all smart enough to see they could go further together for the time being.

You help others. They help you. You are better together. That's how it works. That's how justice gets done.

Still, there is a part of this that can make people uncomfortable. Again, we think that being right is enough. We think merits mean something. Maybe on paper, but not in the arena!

Cato the Younger was famous for his moral uprightness, his incorruptibility. Rome, like the world today, needed more leaders like him. But when Pompey came to him for an alliance, suggesting a marriage between their relatives, which, as it happened, Cato's family supported, Cato rejected it out of hand.

He was confusing incorruptibility with isolationism, and it cost him . . . and Rome. Pompey married Julius Caesar's daughter instead, and soon enough, Caesar, so strengthened, would overthrow the republic. None of this would have happened, Plutarch rightly pointed out, had Cato not "been so afraid of the slight transgressions of Pompey as to allow him to commit the greatest of all, and add his power to that of another."

Stalin was not a good man. He was a necessary ally to win World War II—as the United States understood. Hitler learned this the hard way, driving Russia into the arms of Britain and America—the *Allies*—when he broke the nonaggression pact with Stalin and invaded his former ally.

The side with the most allies usually wins. It's a simple as that.

If we're too pure for this, for friends, for compromise, if we can't keep our word, if we prove too corrupt or selfish or indecent to partner with, then someone else will fill that void—then they'll use that power to advance their interests and not ours, for causes that are not right or just. Who does that serve?

The Stoics would say that we were put here to work with other people—that the ability to collaborate and connect and compromise is in fact one of the things that makes us human. No one is saying this won't be infuriating. That it won't require immense discipline and self-control even to be in the same room with people you'll have to work with—but that's the point, you'll be in the room, working. Not outside, yelling.

The civil rights movement would have unfolded very differently without Louis Martin, a pioneering black journalist turned power broker who advised FDR and famously arranged the phone call from the Kennedys that saved Martin Luther King Jr. from jail (and secured the Kennedys the presidency). It was Martin, working in the Johnson administration, who helped get Thurgood Marshall on the Supreme Court. Johnson was himself quite familiar with the behind-the-scenes genius of someone like Martin, once saying that that was the way you got things done in the world, "you get close to those that are the heads of things."

You can disagree with many of a person's beliefs. You may even hate some of the people you have to ally with.* But to get good things done, you'll have to come together. That's a fact.

It's also a fact that you will come to love some of the people you thought you would hate. Or better, that you might convert to love some of the people who were previously driven by hate. That's the wonderful thing, by allying, by coming together, we *are* bringing justice in the world. By simply working together, Harvey Milk and the Teamsters created a bridge. Men who were admitted homophobes came to know and understand and support an openly gay man. "The union of beer drivers, blacks, Chicanos and Latinos and gays fighting together," Milk

---

* Churchill reminds us, "There is only one thing worse than fighting with allies, and that is fighting without them."

would write, planted the seeds for future justice and, more beautifully, *was* justice embodied.

Let's destroy our enemies by converting them into friends. Let's get enough friends to make it impossible for anyone to destroy us.

We can make the world better by coming together.

By coming together, the world *is* better.

Become Powerful

~

In 416 BC, Melos, a small island in the Aegean Sea, was invaded by Athens, a great foreign power that ruled the Mediterranean. The Athenians did not have much use for the island themselves, but they worried their enemy, the Spartans, might. So as a chess move in the long Peloponnesian War, Athens attacked and demanded submission.

The people of Melos resisted valiantly, but they were outnumbered. The Athenians laid siege and then sent in diplomats to negotiate a surrender.

It was an outrage, the Melians argued, to invade a sovereign country without provocation. They had a right to be neutral. They had a right to be free. How could Athens possibly justify what they were doing?

The men from Athens did not bother to try. "We shall not trouble you with specious pretenses," they explained. They would not make long speeches or pretend what they were doing was fair. They did not try to manufacture a provocation. It was all very simple, they said. This was the way of the world, where "the strong do what they can and the weak suffer what they must."

Talk about saying the quiet part out loud.

The Athenians were saying: We have power. You don't. We can do what we want.

It was awful. It wasn't right. But it was true.

It was also an encapsulation of far too much history before and since.

Power rules the world.

It is very hard to achieve justice without it.

It's very hard to stop injustice without it.

It's very hard to do *anything* without it.

When Robert F. Kennedy took over the Justice Department, he of course believed that civil rights was a moral issue. He knew that racism was a deep-seated prejudice that would take generations to overcome. But he also knew it was a matter of political power. Southern politicians would not be so "fresh" about race in their speeches, Kennedy explained to black leaders, if they had to deal with a significant bloc of black voters in each election. And that was the brilliance of King's protests as well as his voter registration drives. "Not only are we using the tools of persuasion," King said, "but we've got to use the tools of coercion."

Coercion.

That's not exactly the kind of noble sentiment that we remember from the inspiring speeches. But that's what the Montgomery bus boycott was: a raw exercise of black economic power, one that brought the bus system to near insolvency and thus changed the policies, if not the minds, of the operators.

Wasn't that what Clarkson's sugar boycott was about? Wasn't that what he used his political allies in office for? He persuaded with his ideas, but he brought them into being with the power of his coalition and the pressure they applied.

Just as the beneficiaries of slavery and the bankers resisted Clarkson's efforts because it threatened to cost them millions, Martin Luther King Jr. also came to understand there was a reason why Southern sheriffs and governors fought back against him so hard. It was something far beyond preposterous notions about miscegenation or the natural order of things. It's that the racists knew that they were outnumbered. It's that with each voter he registered, he threatened their livelihoods. It's that with each television broadcast, each newspaper story, he chipped away at their control, at the system they had hijacked. They were not just going to let that happen.

Even when the status quo is unjust—in fact, often precisely when the status quo is unjust, there are people who are benefiting from it. Naturally, they're going to resist change.

Nearly everything we see in this world is ultimately explained by this power imbalance. Power is partly why one side of town is pretty and well manicured and the other isn't, it's why one group is bailed out and the other isn't, why some crimes are punished severely and the others get a slap on the wrist, why the rich start the wars but the poor die in them, why some issues are talked about and others aren't—these are all the result of intense power struggles, where someone or something asserted its dominance over another, used the power of coercion to get what it wanted or needed.

Some of these battles were settled—fairly or not—a long time ago, some are still raging right now. It is never preordained that justice will prevail. It is, however, almost certain that justice will not prevail without power.

Good ideas, good causes, fair notions—they are not just adopted automatically. More often than not, they have to be rammed down people's throats. Leverage must be acquired. An overwhelming coalition of allies must be assembled. Walls have to be breached. Resistance has to be crushed.

Change is scary! It means winners and losers. It involves dollars and cents, perks and privileges.

"Reports are not self-executive," Florence Nightingale would remind herself and her staff. Just because you knew what needed to be done, just because you had cogently argued for the right and fair and desperately necessary solution, just because innocent lives depended on it didn't mean it was going to happen. No, you needed competence to execute . . . and you needed friends in high places. You needed funding. You needed public support. You needed to be able to force it through.

Most of all, you needed power.

Too many activists think there is something noble about

being outsiders. They think the whole system is corrupt. They think the system *is* the problem. They're not wrong—there are real problems. But because of their idealism and purity they're not able to do anything about those problems, and so they themselves are part of the problem all the same. It's very hard to change that system from a distance.

Even presidents and prime ministers find this out. They get elected, but they forget that if their parties don't also control the legislative bodies, if they don't have a mandate from voters, if they can't get leverage over a handful of other power brokers, their agenda is dead in the water.

"Power per se is nothing bad. It is necessary," Angela Merkel would explain. "Power is 'to make'—to do something. The opposite of power is powerless. What's the use of a good idea if I can't execute it?"

The opposite of power is powerlessness.

Is that what you want?

You can resign in protest. You can call them all bastards. You can damn the whole world as corrupt and broken. Just know that, in so doing, you may put yourself out of the running to be of service to anything but your sense of superiority.

The question to ask is: Who does *not* having power serve? What good does that do?

Anyone who wants to do good in this world must be a student of power. Anyone who wants to do something other than sit around and wait for change must read Machiavelli and

Robert Greene. They must study the campaigns of the great leaders who got things done . . . as well as the demagogues and tyrants who did evil things. They must know how to effectively gain and use power as well as how to defend against it. How to acquire allies, how to use them, how to get things done over objections and entrenched interests. In fact, the more averse to power one is, the more likely one needs to get up close and personal about it—before their naivete or idealism brings them or their cause harm.

Seneca's life illustrates this tricky balance. He came to work for Nero, doing his best to be "in the room where it happens" so he could moderate Nero's excesses and try to lead the empire in a positive direction. He also grew extremely rich in this service and slowly became complicit in the administration's misdeeds, staining his hands in the process. Power corrupts, as we know. It's a dangerous tool. We can't covet it for its own sake . . . but we also can't ignore it and hope for the best.*

The fact of the matter is that bullies like Athens exist. Not just in the past but right now (just ask Ukraine). They are the source of pain and injustice. A world with countervailing powers, a world where the good guys unilaterally disarm? That is not a better world. It's a world where the strong do what they like and the weak suffer.

---

* Other Stoics like Arius Didymus (who tutored Augustus) and Posidonius (who advised Scipio Aemilianus) seemed to do better.

That's not right. That's not keeping your hands clean.

Besides, it's fully possible to do both.

In 1860, as he sought the presidency and the South sought the expansion of slavery—an institution built around dominance but made possible by its political and economic base—Abraham Lincoln spoke at Cooper Union in New York City, urging Republicans to step up their fight, to not be intimidated. They needed the power to stop the passage of new laws, they needed lawyers to argue in the courts, they needed to appoint the judges who would control the courts, they might well soon need soldiers in the field. "Neither let us be slandered from our duty by false accusations against us, nor frightened from it by menaces of destruction to the Government nor of dungeons to ourselves," he said. And then he continued, raising his voice in steely determination:

> LET US HAVE FAITH THAT RIGHT MAKES MIGHT, AND IN THAT FAITH, LET US, TO THE END, DARE TO DO OUR DUTY AS WE UNDERSTAND IT.

The courage to bring force against force, power against power, is no small thing. Indeed, it is the only thing that power respects. And now that we have it, let's use it to do what's right.

Practice Pragmatism

⁓

Jimmy Carter did the right thing on inauguration day in 1971. It didn't cost him much as a governor because in Georgia at that time it was a single-term job.

Six years after his stunning speech in Georgia, he was elected president of the United States. On his very first day in office, just hours after his inauguration parade, he held a 4:35p.m. meeting—literally his first appointment—with a disabled army veteran named Max Cleland to discuss another stunning announcement. After asking Cleland, who'd lost both legs and an arm in the Battle of Khe Sanh, to head the Veterans Administration, Carter instructed him to begin working on a blanket pardon for everyone who had evaded serving in Vietnam. It would "heal the nation's wounds," allow Americans stuck in Canada to come home, allow people to come out of hiding and remove shame and stigma. He believed the time for forgiveness and understanding had come.

Cleland, who supported the idea, warned the president that

it would be unpopular in the Senate and might be worth delay-ing, perhaps until his second term. "I don't care if all 100 of them are against me," Carter replied. "It's the right thing to do."

And then he did it—second term be damned.

As it happened, despite what was actually a surprisingly ef-fective presidency, Carter would not get a second term, losing in a landslide in 1980 to Ronald Reagan, a defeat some trace to that decision he made on his first day in office.

Carter always said that he never wanted to do anything to hurt his country—that's why he refused to delay doing the right thing. Still, his wife, Rosalynn, tried to explain that not getting reelected would hurt the country. And it's a thought that's haunted his supporters ever since: What could Carter have done with another four years in office, with another four years of power?

Why did he have to tackle giving the Panama Canal back to its rightful owners or peace in the Middle East in his first term? Could he have accomplished more if he'd been a little more pragmatic? A little less idealistic? Could he have played the game a little better?

The reality is that people who get things done have to be both.

People who knew Harvey Milk before and during his first unsuccessful run for office in 1973 were shocked to see him in the next campaign. He had cut off his long hair to appear more respectable. The Harvey Milk who eventually won office in 1977 was even more unrecognizable. He'd stopped smoking pot. He'd cut off his mustache and started wearing dapper business suits.

That's one of the ways you get allies—by looking like someone they can do business with. You could argue that this is unfair, that appearances shouldn't matter, that people should be able to dress and behave however they want, that the only thing that should matter is a person's character and the righteousness of their cause.

And guess what? In arguing this you are proving the very real need for pragmatism.

Because we're not talking about how things *should* be. We're talking about how they *are*. This is a real condition in front of us, not a theory. A fact, not a hypothetical.

As such, the way forward for Harvey Milk was quite clear. "I decided this was all too important," he explained, "to have it get wrecked because of smoking a joint or being in a raid at some bathhouse."

What you're doing is important—important enough that you have got to be pragmatic about it.

If there was ever a cause good enough to deserve success on its merits, it would have been the passage of the Thirteenth Amendment, which would permanently and irrevocably end slavery in America forever. Four years of war had led up to it. Hundreds of thousands of soldiers had perished.

Lincoln knew that he was on the right side of the issue, that "if slavery is not wrong, nothing is wrong." But that didn't change the fact that he was painfully short on the votes needed to pass it. Lincoln didn't solve this problem by giving another Gettysburg Address. He did not appeal to the public's better angels. The politician of more than two decades got to work. He horse-traded. He logrolled. He applied pressure. "I'll leave it to you to determine how it shall be done," he said to his lobbyists. "I am the President of the United States, clothed with immense power, and I expect you to procure those two votes."*

It wasn't pretty, but it did the job, not just for those then held in bondage but for millions still unborn.

Justice can be beautifully articulated by a moralist. It is unlikely, however, that they will ever be able to bring such a thing about.

What justice needs is not only the honesty and incorruptibility of Harry Truman, but also his ability to survive inside the machine, to get things done. There is a tension between these ideas, to be sure, as Truman well knew. At one agonizing moment, to pass a bond issue Truman had to ignore the fact that one of his fellow judges had stolen about $10,000, if he had any hope of preventing that same man from stealing over $1 million from the taxpayers. "Was I right or did I compound a felony?" Truman would muse in a deeply private bit of writing. "I don't know . . . I've got the $6,500,000 worth of roads on the ground

---

* The beauty of Lincoln, one of his political mentors noted, was that he was a master trader of favors yet he "refused to be sold. *He never had a price.*"

and at a figure that makes the crooks tear their hair. . . . Am I an administrator or not? Or am I just a crook to compromise in order to get the job done? You judge it, I can't."

Pragmatism without virtue is dangerous and hollow. Virtue without pragmatism is ineffectual and impotent.

Charles de Gaulle explained that it wasn't just raw courage that was required to lead, but that a statesman "must know when to dissemble, when to be frank. . . . Every man of action has a strong dose of egotism, pride, hardness and cunning. But all those things will be forgiven of him—indeed they will be regarded as high qualities—if he can make them the means to achieve great ends."

That sounds a little Machiavellian, doesn't it?

Good!

Machiavelli wasn't the bad guy that idealists make him out to be. He was as principled as they come—in fact, he was brutally tortured for his role in attempt to keep his country free. He was also a realist and he understood that the good, matched as they were against evil, would need to be both a lion *and* a fox if they would have any hope of bringing good into the world. That is, brave *and* savvy.

The ends don't always justify the means . . . but what does failing to achieve your ends justify? Is that justice? The reality is that injustice and inhumanity often have an economic logic to them. They have interests behind them. The triumph of the good cannot be left to the ineffectual, the unrealistic, or the naive. Not when the enemy is evil, aggressive, protean, and indefatigable.

Kant famously said that a person shouldn't ever lie—even if a murderer is beating on your door asking where your children are. It doesn't sound like someone you'd want answering the door on your behalf, does it? That doesn't sound like a person who cares very much about the people in their care—it sounds like they care about rigid principles more than real people. It sounds like the attitude that the murderer—or your political opponents—would like you to have. Because it paralyzes. Makes someone a sitting, ineffectual duck.

An idealogue or a philosopher can be pure. A leader has to make decisions. A leader has to take action. They must be an idealist as well as a realist. Because they have things they have to protect. They can't turn up their nose at a crumb—not when their people are hungry. They can't afford to judge a potential ally or insist on perfect messengers. They must take the world, the situation, as it is, not as they would like it to be—especially if they want to change it. They can't let a hypothetical interfere with an opportunity to help, right here, right now. The fact that they can't solve *all* the problems is not an excuse for not solving *some* of them. Standing on principle is one thing, but too easily we can find ourselves standing on something much flimsier, much more self-indulgent or symbolic.

Especially when other people are at stake.

Each of us will have to figure out how to strike this balance in each individual scenario. Take the inspiring, courageous stand of August Landmesser, captured in that photo, the lone man refusing to give the Nazi salute. Dietrich Bonhoeffer, who would be executed for conspiring to assassinate Hitler, would have agreed with the sentiment but taken issue with a such a pure but ultimately ineffectual stand. Despite his deep Christian piety and abiding disgust for all aspects of Nazism, when he saw one of his collaborators refuse to give the salute, he asked if they were crazy. "Raise your arm!" he said. "We'll have to run risks for many things, but this silly salute is not one of them."

When you know what your north star is, you have the ability to make these kinds of decisions. It doesn't mean that every means is justified because you have an end, but it does give you clarity, some wiggle room, some ability to prioritize. Following a north star does not mean you walk into falls and wade into rushing rivers—a skilled navigator learns how to be directionally correct while not crashing into things or killing themselves. This should not be a controversial statement in the pursuit of justice.

Politics, building things, making things happen—it's dirty, dusty business. We cannot wait for perfect men, nor can we pretend to be pure ourselves. Doing good in this world is not going to be easy. It will not be without its opponents or obstacles. We can call them names. We can despair. We can blame.

Or we can get to work.

Non angeli sed angli.

Stop looking for angels. Start looking for angles.

But let's go back to Carter for a second. This was a man who was pragmatic enough to tell civil rights leaders that they wouldn't like his campaign but they would like his administration—he knew that some things were a means to an end. Was his decision to tackle such a hot-button issue on his first day in office naive and reckless? Some think so. But another read is that it was also quite pragmatic.

None of us know how long we have—in life, in power, in a certain moment of time. No one can tell you for certain that by putting something off, you'll have a better shot down the road.* No one can tell you for certain that you *will* be reelected. Which is why most of the time the pragmatic choice is to do the right thing, right now.

When you have the shot you have to take it.

People are counting on you.

---

* One unpopular thing Carter did in his first term was issuing an executive order mandating seatbelts and airbags. Whether that was idealistic or pragmatic, there are literally millions of people alive today because of that decision.

Develop Competence

~

Florence Nightingale got off to a slow start. Her pioneering, world-changing career in nursing was long underground, taking nearly twenty years to go from "The Call," as she famously spoke of it, to her service on the front lines of the troop hospitals in Crimea.

But this time was hardly lost. In fact, it was a kind of slow-motion training montage, a long apprenticeship in an unappreciated art.

First, there was her exploration—groundbreaking in that era—of whether it was possible for a woman to pursue any kind of calling. She asked for advice. She looked for mentors and patrons. Next, she nursed sick relatives, starting with her grandmother, as well as villagers near where she lived. And then, finally, she volunteered in hospitals in Germany and France, where she experienced firsthand not just the pressures of the sick ward but the dire and disastrous state of nursing at that time.

"I saw a poor woman die before my eyes this summer,"

Nightingale would write to a friend in 1845, "because there was nothing but fools to sit up with her, who poisoned her as much as if they had given her arsenic." The strange assumption at that time was that a woman of her status should not sully herself with something as coarse as helping the sick or indigent directly . . . and yet it was equally taken for granted that every woman was naturally qualified and skilled at nursing by nature of her sex.

Just as with the long-held belief that firstborn sons from prestigious families were fit by birth to lead troops or hold office, there was almost no basis for this stereotype. On the contrary! And that's what struck Nightingale most—the *gross incompetence* of the nurses, as well as the doctors. They may have meant well, but they had no idea what they were doing . . . which in the end meant that meaning well meant nothing.

"It may seem a strange principle to enunciate as the very first requirement in a Hospital that it should do the sick no harm," Nightingale would explain. "It is quite necessary nevertheless to lay down such a principle, because the actual mortality in hospitals, especially those of large crowded cities, is very much higher than any calculator found on the mortality of the same class of patient treated out of hospital would lead us to expect."

Because they were so confidently incompetent, they not only didn't help, they killed people. Graveyards full of them. All the while patting themselves on the back for their compassion and dedication.

Longfellow's famous poem would portray Nightingale as a kind of angel, gliding through the halls of her hospital, comforting the sick and the dying. It was a beautiful image.

It is not correct.

A more accurate picture of Nightingale would show her as a stern teacher of other nurses—a trainer who developed a generation of talent so they could treat and comfort the wounded. We should picture her late at night, leaning over her desk reading reports, writing letters to politicians and generals, ordering supplies, fighting for resources. We should imagine her tinkering with how the hospital ran, solving problems, making things more sanitary and efficient.'

"The public generally imagine her by the soldier's bedside," Nightingale's aunt and colleague would write back to their family in 1855. "How easy, how satisfactory if it were all. The quantity of the writing, the quantity of talking is the weary work, the dealing with the mean, the selfish, the incompetent."

More than devotion, she understood that patients needed clean beds. More than self-sacrifice, they needed nutritious meals and working heaters. Instead of asking her nurses to be angels, Nightingale studied the traffic flow of the hospital and designed a better communication system—using a series of bells so patients could ring for help—that meant less time running up and down stairs and thus more time providing care. She fought for better ventilation. She brought in donations from the public by the thousand.

And then with this money, she was a diligent and skilled steward. During the Second World War, a government auditor would review the Army Medical Services accounting system and find it impressively efficient and accurate. When they asked who had designed it, they were shocked to find that it had been Florence Nightingale some *eighty years* earlier—another of her thankless innovations and improvements.

Of course, to do good one has to care—caring really matters. But it's like that expression about wishing in one hand, shitting the other. Which one fills up first? Emoting at the people or causes that are suffering? Same goes for that other expression about the road to hell being paved with good intentions. What justice needs is time, money, leadership. What they need is *someone who knows what they're doing.*

Can you be that person? Someone competent, someone who approaches justice not as an idea but as a craft. As an occupation to always be getting better at.

Competence is not a birthright, nor does it automatically attend a cause just because the cause is right. Compassion is necessary but not sufficient in the pursuit of justice. Courage and discipline too—necessary but pointless without aptitude.

One could argue that the Carter presidency struggled not because of Carter's bold and brave stands but because he refused to hire a White House Chief of Staff, contrary to all advice. He was a good man but had trouble managing all the demands on his time and attention. The sociologist and philosopher Max Weber once described political change as the "slow boring of hard boards." Pragmatism is competence. So is determination and delegation. Competence is competence and there is no substitute for it. It took Nightingale years to understand the problem she was trying to solve, but then years more to fight through the resistance and obstacles in order to implement solutions. And then after that came the life-and-death difficulties of treating wounded patients in a war zone.

But that's how it goes. It's not for the faint of heart. It's not for the inept either.

Think of Truman—the Marshall Plan was not just brilliantly named after Marshall to give the political opposition cover to vote for it. He then made sure the money and aid was also offered to Soviet countries—which all declined, but it undermined any communist argument that the plan was self-interested. The "unsordid act," as Winston Churchill called it, wasn't pure, it was brilliantly and cunningly rolled out. So too were Roosevelt's efforts during the Depression—it wasn't simply that he was courageous or caring, it's that he made the political system *work*. He wielded the levers of power effectively, actively, in a way that they have never been used before or since.

"The most pervasive mistake I have made was in believing that because our cause was just, we could be sure that the white ministers of the South, once their Christian consciences were challenged, would rise to our aid." Martin Luther King Jr. once said. He came to understand that righteousness without skilled organizing, action without strategy was a recipe for letting the cause down. What he became, with the help of Bayard Rustin, Stanley Levison, Diane Nash, Ella Baker, was a political and media force to be reckoned with. And then he combined that force with Lyndon B. Johnson, who while more racist and less idealistic than Kennedy, was a legislative genius. Johnson understood power—where to find it, how to use it—and this power, added to King's, made the two an unstoppable force for good.

It is a model for all who want to bring good into the world, however big or small.

"I try to emulate all the saints of history," King would say, adding though that "it's necessary for anyone who is working in these areas to have a keen sense of political training." Certainly Theodore Roosevelt came to understand this. After he discovered how the other half lived and set about attacking various corrupt interests, he was repeatedly foiled by his opponents' superior understanding of parliamentary maneuvers as well as the judges and reporters under their control. His friend Jacob Riis would say that "honesty was not enough." To eventually change the political and economic landscape of the country, Roosevelt would have to not just be right, but be savvier and more skilled than those who wished to stop him.

So will you.

It doesn't matter that the writer has something important to say, what counts is whether they have the chops to communicate it to the reader. It doesn't matter that a politician has all the right positions. Do they know how the system works, do they have the staff, do they have the relationships to get it done? It doesn't matter that the lawyer is willing to take the case. Can they win it? It doesn't matter that someone *feels bad* for the vulnerable or the afflicted, or even that they work really hard on their behalf. What counts is whether this effort is actually alleviating that suffering, not temporarily but permanently.

Nor is justice simply about political acumen and people skills. Strength is important too—raw physical power, resources, the ability to win. There are bad guys in this world . . . and those bad guys are often strong, often violent, often in command of serious power that they use to inflict their will on others. Who will stand up to them? Who is strong enough to *stop* them?

We can't just mean well. We have to be able to *do* well.

What does it say about humanity that *effective* altruism is a new concept?

Every problem must be studied. Every skill must be practiced. Every variable necessary for success—allies, funding, public support, power—must be cultivated. Impact must be measured. Decisions must be optimized. People must be held accountable. We have to hold ourselves accountable—that's how we get better.

This will take time. In Nightingale's case, it took *years* for her to turn her raw potential into rock-hard competence. This will require learning by trial and error, as King did in his failed campaigns in St. Augustine and other cities. It will require courage, discipline, and wisdom.

Of course it will. If change, if being of service was easy, everyone would do it. If problems solved themselves, there wouldn't be problems. The world would be fair and wonderful and the right people would always be in charge.

Until then?

Until then we have to be smart and capable and competent.

Give, Give, Give

~

W hen Rabbi Harold Kushner sat down to write a book, he tried not to procrastinate. He tried to get right into it—no hesitation, no overthinking.

He allowed only one small ritual to precede his act of daily discipline.

Before his pen touched to the page or the notepad, it went first to his checkbook, where Kushner scrawled out a small donation to one of the charities that he and his wife supported. In the way that the ancients might have prepared for battle with a sacrifice to the gods or the muses, the rabbi waged the war of art by first striking with an act of kindness. He warmed up for a day of good writing by writing down some numbers he knew would do some good.

Generosity is something we admire. It's something many of us wish we could be better at.

As it happens, there's only one way to get there, to do that. And it's the same way one gets better at writing or any other craft: *by doing it.*

Not later, when we're better off. Not only when somebody really needs it. Not in one or two big or flashy moments.

But consistently, regularly, as a matter of course. So it becomes part of who we are. So it becomes a kind of north star in and of itself.

Anne Frank's motto, which she learned from her parents, is that "no one ever became poor by giving." It's true, charity is edifying and profoundly rewarding. And as it happens, the Hebrew word for charity—*tzedakah*—means "justice."

Of course, there's some part of us that does know that giving money away is a good way to go broke. Plus, we hustled and sweated and earned what we have. We know how money might compound and grow if properly invested. And we can't help but think about the fun things we could do with it—or some moment in the distant future when we might badly need it.

Yet aren't all these also reasons to be generous with it? We worked hard because it was our job, because we wanted to realize our potential. The financial compensation is something we are glad to get but also understand is extra. We earned it once, we can earn it again. And what kind of person values their fun— or redundant security—over the alleviation of someone else's suffering?

If you've been blessed, be a blessing.

And there, it should be said, are many ways to do this.

We can be generous with our time, as Florence Nightingale was, dedicating her life to service instead of high society. We can be generous with credit, generous with praise. We can be the kind of person whom people come to for help, the kind of person whose door is always open, the kind of person who smiles at strangers, who fixes friends up, who checks on people who are lonely, who is there when you need them with a nice word. We can use our power and influence to fight for people who have little, as Theodore Roosevelt did. We can be generous with our access and advice.

Kindness is a form of generosity we can always afford.

It doesn't matter how much money you have, how much power you have (or how little), nothing is stopping you from being generous in some form or some way. *How are you doing? Do you need anything? Great job. I appreciate you.* These are expressions of generosity that don't cost a thing.

Nothing is stopping you from being generous *right now.* The immensity of the problems or the needs of the world do not absolve you or prevent you from making a small step toward solving them, doing *something* for someone who is suffering from them.

During the Depression, wanderers and hobos would often stop at the Carter house, which was not far from the railroad tracks. Carter's mother would always fix them something to eat. One neighbor noted how thankful she was that there were never any of *them* hanging around her house. Later, Jimmy Carter would learn that the community of homeless people during the Depression had a series of symbols to communicate which houses were decent and kind and which were heartless and cruel and to be avoided.

The idea of this mark—of *earning* it from those in need—stayed with Carter all his life. It's why into his nineties he was donating his time and money to help others, even building houses for those who could not afford their own.

It's funny, Ralph Waldo Emerson is famous for his essays on self-reliance, but in reality he was an incredibly generous man—not just with his money but with his time and his encouragement. The scene he cultivated in Massachusetts has no parallel in history. People all over New England knew they were welcomed at Emerson's home, where unofficial meetings naturally began forming what later historians came to call the Transcendental Club. He mentored and helped forge the careers of countless artists and intellectuals. It was, after all, on Emerson's land at Walden Pond that Thoreau was allowed to live and build his cabin. He supported his family members financially. Emerson was an unstoppable champion of education—a vocal and financial supporter of public libraries and access to knowledge. Great, Emerson later said, is the person who confers the most benefits. The more successful you are, the more self-reliant you are, the more left over you have to help others become the same.

To whom much is given, much is expected.

And we have been given so much, each of us. All of us.

What will we do with it? Who will we help? What will we give?

An answer: *Enough that it hurts. Enough that it challenges us. Enough that there is sacrifice in it.*

Why should we get to keep it all to ourselves anyway? It's not really ours to begin with. Who owns the patent on your vaccine, Jonas Salk was asked on television as he rolled out the first protections against the scourge of polio. "Well, the people, I would say," he answered, aware as he was that his research had been funded by charitable donations and built on the backs of so many other scientific breakthroughs. "There is no patent. Could you patent the sun?"

Marcus Aurelius, reflecting on the whole of his life, would write that he felt lucky to have never needed to ask for money but luckier still that whenever anyone else needed it, he was never in a position to have to say he couldn't afford to help.

It's not only the right and fair thing to do, but it makes us great.

So we must make a start of it, a habit of it.

The point is not how or how much, it's that we *are* a blessing to others—in whatever form we can be, in whatever way is possible.

Grow a Coaching Tree

B y all-time wins, Gregg Popovich is perhaps the greatest coach in the history of the NBA. When one adds to that his number of championships (five), his number of winning seasons (twenty-two), his unbroken streak of playoff appearances (twenty-two), his winning percentage (.657), his Olympic gold medals (two), and the fact that he did it all with one team, he may well be the greatest coach in the history of the game of basketball.

But there is another metric besides wins and rings—less considered, but more important—that could make the case for him as the greatest coach in sports: his coaching tree.

In sports, a coaching tree is defined by the coaches and players and executives that a coach has discovered, hired, and mentored and what they go on to do in their careers. Gregg Popovich's coaching tree is so extensive, as one sportswriter put it, that it's actually more like a *coaching forest.*

In the course of becoming the longest-tenured coach in *all* of the major professional sports leagues, Gregg Popovich would take under his wing multiple Hall of Fame players like Tim Duncan and Tony Parker and Manu Ginóbili, who not only made up one of the great dynasties in the modern NBA but stayed in San Antonio and became leaders in their community. At one point, nearly 30 percent of *all* the coaches in the NBA had worked for or played under Popovich, and his protégés have, independently, won eleven championships as head coaches (and one G League championship). Five times, someone from his forest has been named the NBA Coach of the Year. Of the current twenty-three black head coaches and GMs in the NBA, seven spent time under Popovich at the Spurs. Becky Hammon, the 2022 WNBA Head Coach of the Year, spent eight years with the Spurs, where she was the first female assistant coach in the NBA and the first to serve as an acting head coach after an ejected Popovich designated her his replacement (she won two-straight WNBA titles as a coach too). And if one were to begin to trace out the coaching trees from the coaches in Popovich's coaching tree, you would touch nearly everyone in NBA and NCAA basketball.

It was this thought that struck Adam Silver, the commissioner of the NBA, during the 2022 Finals, which pitted two coaches whom Popovich had coached, hired, and mentored against each other. The Spurs were more than just a basketball team, he said, they were practically an *academy* for future coaches and team executives.

"Let the honor of your students be as dear to you as your own," Rabbi Eleizer famously said. But this is a little easier when you're a teacher—because that's *the job*. If Popovich was running an academy—a nonprofit, mission-based educational organization—these accomplishments would be quite impressive. The fact that he managed to do this while operating at the highest level of a cutthroat game where he's actually helping, if not producing, his competition? This is something he has done outside his commitment to winning, both as an ideal and as an expectation of his employment. This is not the "old boys club" either, with a bunch of people scratching each other's backs, or one leader making identical replicas of themselves. No it's the act of opening a door, extending a ladder to a diverse group of unique leaders, different types of athletes, coaches, and executives as they reach to fulfill their potential.

So as you look at your career, it bears asking:

Who have you given a shot?

Who have you helped get ahead?

More revealing, how similar to you or unlike you were these people?

Yet far too often, we are more interested in how to get someone to give *us* a shot. Or how to get another one or a bigger one or a better one. We think that by helping others we jeopardize ourselves, as if life or work was zero-sum.

Highlander syndrome says, *There can only be one.*

No, there is room for all of us to succeed. For far more to succeed than currently are.

George Marshall advanced in his career, was able to get to

the top of his profession and do well there, precisely because he understood that his job was to help other people—to build an army full of talented officers. While other generals fought tooth and nail for their own advancement, wrote letters to their superiors lobbying for promotions or choice assignments, Marshall was advocating for promising young men like Omar Bradley, George Patton, Walter Krueger, and most of all, Dwight D. Eisenhower, whom he nurtured into history-defining talents. His coaching tree, you might say, was the oak upon which the Allied victory depended.

In this life, of course, we are measured by our accomplishments as individuals. We strive to realize our potential and do our best. But after a certain point, this only means so much. What matters more, what matters over a longer horizon, is who we have helped succeed along the way.

To be clear, it's not just sports where a coaching tree counts. Socrates brought us Alcibiades and Xenophon and Plato. Plato in turn brought us Aristotle, and Aristotle, Alexander.

Emerson not only generously supported the literary scene in New England, but actively encouraged talent wherever he encountered it. "I greet you at the beginning of a great career," Emerson gushed in a letter to a struggling Walt Whitman in 1855 (which Whitman promptly added as a blurb to the front of his then undiscovered, self-published masterpiece *Leaves of Grass*). Without Emerson the careers of Nathaniel Hawthorne, William Ellery Channing, Amos Bronson Alcott, and later William

James (Emerson's godson) and Alcott's daughter Louisa May Alcott would have gone very differently. Generosity is the seed of a great coaching tree.

Thomas Wentworth Higginson, in addition to his work as an abolitionist, helped mentor and publish the poetry of Emily Dickinson. Frederick Douglass encouraged and mentored Ida B. Wells, whose antilynching work as well as her work for women's suffrage and in helping to found the NAACP in 1909 were brilliant extensions of the legacy of Douglass, a man born into slavery in 1818. Martin Luther King Jr.'s legacy is also burnished by the fact that John Lewis went on to become a congressman, Andrew Young became ambassador to the UN, and Diane Nash won the Presidential Medal of Freedom.

Denzel Washington paid for Chadwick Boseman to go to college. Walker Percy was adopted by his uncle Will, and then he in turn was a quiet mentor and teacher to the biographer Walter Isaacson. Percy also discovered and helped publish, posthumously, John Kennedy Toole's Pulitzer Prize–winning novel *A Confederacy of Dunces*. George Carlin met a young Garry Shandling in a comedy club in Arizona in 1968, and after he read Shandling's jokes notebook said, "I think you're funny. . . . If you're thinking of pursuing it, I think you should."* Shandling in turn would mentor the director Judd Apatow, Kevin Nealon,

---

* Carlin would often close his act with a reminder along similar lines: "Take care of yourself and take care of somebody else too."

Adam Sandler, and Sarah Silverman, alongside a generation of comedic talent of the '80s, '90s, and 2000s.

And what of the people these trailblazers never met but whom their work influenced, whom their example inspired? This is true multigenerational impact, an infinite web of butterfly wings flapped, of lives changed and better futures written.

That's the thing. Not all of us have the power to change or improve the world within our own lifetimes. By supporting, encouraging, and influencing others—including our own children—our efforts can live on.

Mentor. Patron. Sponsor. Ally. Teacher. Master. Guru. Inspiration.

There are so many names for it . . . because it's a role defined by so many different roles.

But what matters is that we are the candle that lights another, which lights another, which lights another.

Because through this whole worlds are illuminated, delivered from darkness.

Look Out for the Little Guy

A ngela Merkel grew up in the shadow of the evils that her country had committed. She also grew up a pastor's daughter, living alongside a charity their church ran for the mentally handicapped, seeing the Sermon on the Mount in action. It was the latter that defined her worldview. "Malachi sees the violence in society against the weak," she said, paraphrasing the Bible, "those who are at the margin of society, the hired workers, the widows and the orphans treated unjustly. Malachi says that this is unacceptable; it goes against God's commandments. . . . The weakest in society must not be wronged. We must focus our attention on them."

What was the only example of Jesus losing his temper? It was over the money changers—the den of thieves—who had taken over the temple. They were price gouging. They were harming society.

It was this version of Christianity, the one that emphasized the story of the Good Samaritan, the one that cared for the "bruised reeds" of the world, that colored Merkel's decision to accept one *million* refugees fleeing the Syrian civil war that began in 2011. You'd think other Christian nations would have rushed to follow suit, but no, she was widely criticized, the plight of these suffering masses reduced to some political or cultural debate, as if these were not human beings who could and must be helped.

Yet she pushed forward anyway. *Wir schaffen das,* she reassured the public. We can do this.

We can.

We must!

If we're not going to fight for the little guy, do what we can for them, who will? And if we allow them to be hurt or exploited or left to suffer, *what does that say about us?*

From an early age, Cato disliked bullies. At a birthday party for a friend, a group of boys were playing a Roman version of the game cops and robbers. One of the younger boys was caught and shut into a dark chamber by one of the older boys. Scared, the child called for Cato, who threw aside the boy blocking the door and took the scared child home to his parents. As a teenager, he was invited with his tutor to the house of Sulla, who then ruled Rome as a cruel dictator. As the tutor explained to Cato why everyone feared Sulla, he watched Cato's entire countenance change. "Why don't you give me a sword," Cato said with total sincerity, "so that I could free my country from slavery?" And as he got older, that's why he hated the corruption in Rome's provinces, because it victimized the inhabitants who deserved better.

Cato and many of the Stoics had a north star that pointed them into opposition to anyone who tried to tell them or anyone what to do—anyone who abused power and wielded it against the weak. In fact, the expression *sic semper tyrannis* (thus always to tyrants) traces itself all the way to Scipio Aemilianus, one of the great Stoic generals before the turn of the millennium.

George Washington, who modeled himself on Cato his entire life, tried to look at every situation with Cato's dispassion, through *the calm light of mild philosophy.* But his view on justice, on the goal of a good government, a just world, was captured in a line that he borrowed from the scriptures: "Every one shall sit in safety under his own vine and fig tree and there shall be none to make him afraid."*

Washington's beautiful evocations of the vine and the fig tree came in 1790, when he spoke to a Jewish congregation in Rhode Island of a vision of America that gave "bigotry no sanction" and "persecution no assistance."

He was talking about tolerance. He was talking about protection. He was talking about diversity and love and hope.

Tyrants, bullies, and jerks are the enemies of justice. They cannot be accepted. They cannot be accommodated. Whether it's an online mob or an economic system that exploits the im-

---

*It's worth pointing out that Washington was morally blind to the race of people who very much did not have the safety of their own vine and fig tree in America at that time.

poverished, the belittling, bullying boss or government that persecutes dissidents or exploits its citizens, tyranny is tyranny.

It puts us all at risk.

After one of the terrible bombings during the civil rights movement, the journalist Ralph McGill wrote an editorial for the *Atlanta Constitution* that put it perfectly. "When the wolves of hate are loosed on one people," he explained, "then no one is safe." The activists themselves, even as they were fighting for their own lives, understood this—that's why Jews came down South in 1964 and were beaten on behalf of blacks, why black leaders spoke out against Vietnam and persecution abroad. "We cannot sit complacently by the wayside while our Jewish brothers in the Soviet Union face the possible extinction of their cultural and spiritual life," Martin Luther King Jr. said in 1966. "Those that sit at rest, while others take pains, are tender turtles and buy their quiet with disgrace.... The denial of human rights anywhere is a threat to the affirmation of human rights everywhere."

We should be sympathetic to the bruised reeds of the world *because we are one.* We too were once strangers in the land of Egypt. We may well be one again someday.

We must see ourselves in the *other.*

The world is unfair and cruel. Do we contribute to that? Or alleviate it?

When we have power—which we all do as a collective—we have to make sure we use it for good.

"Society cannot trample on the weakest and feeblest of its members without receiving the curse in its own soul," Frances Watkins said after she described that great bundle of humanity we are all a part of. Our job is to create a world where people have the opportunity to flourish—spiritually, professionally, personally. Where no one is trampled, where people are encouraged to reach their potential. To thrive and be happy. To follow their own north star. To love who they want. To worship as they want. To think what they want and say what they want.

Across his long career, Clarence Darrow worked with almost every large corporation and interest in the country, even if they weren't always the most benevolent of clients. Businesses are important and they shouldn't be picked on either. But he was also quite firm about one stance, insisting that he never would and never had "given them aid to oppress the weak or convict the innocent." The pivotal moment of his career, in fact, came when he walked away from a lucrative job for the railroads to fight *against* his former clients, who were in a major dispute with labor organizers.

We don't punch down . . . and we don't tolerate others who do it either.

This is why Emerson supported and shielded the Underground Railroad. We not only don't sanction bigotry or give aid to persecution, we do the opposite. We fight against bigotry, we help those who are being persecuted.

Thus always . . .

Are you supporting David or Goliath? Are you fighting against tyranny or are you the tyrant? Are you a truth-teller or are you actually a troll?

Freedom is essential . . . but the most essential freedom is the freedom from fear.

Our job is to fight to make sure the vulnerable are protected and can live without fear.

Because they are us and we are them.

Make Good Trouble

A rthur Ashe was one of the world's best-behaved athletes. While other tennis players threw fits and had affairs, while they broke racquets and drove fancy cars, he was self-contained and dignified. They chased money, he went to West Point and served his country. They were driven, he was disciplined.

It's not that he was passive or apolitical. It was simply that he had learned, from his father's example, not to let his emotions get the best of him—to work quietly but firmly on his goals without drawing unnecessary attention to himself.

So you can imagine Ashe's father's surprise in January 1985 when Arthur called him to say, "Daddy, I want you to know that I'm probably going to be arrested tomorrow, in Washington." In an instant, his father knew this was about apartheid, a cause that their family, having lived in segregated Virginia, knew personally. "Well, son," he said, "South Africa's an awful long way from us here. But if you think you have to do it, then I guess you have to do it."

"I have to do it, Daddy," Arthur replied. The next day, Ashe, the Wimbledon, Australian Open, and U.S. Open champion and captain of the U.S. Davis Cup team, was arrested alongside nearly fifty public school teachers in front of the South African embassy.

It surprised his fans and upset his sponsors. So it goes. Most change, most justice is inherently disruptive. It means challenging how things are. It means upsetting people. It means taking risks. It means saying things that are impolite, unpleasant, and even offensive.

But when you know how the other half lives, when you know there is preventable suffering or state-sanctioned injustice out there—well, you don't care about niceties as much anymore.

As a young man, John Lewis saw the same signs that still existed when Arthur Ashe was a boy. The ones that said "Whites" and "Colored"—signs that separated the world, signs that were tinged with the implicit threat of deadly violence. When he would ask his parents and grandparents what these signs meant, they would tell him, "That's the way it is. Don't get in the way. Don't get in trouble." *Don't upset the order of things. It's not safe. It's not worth it.*

But then Rosa Parks came along. With incredible courage and discipline, she challenged those signs, doing what she thought was right. Years later, Lewis would explain how her example inspired him to "find a way, to get in the way, to get in what I call good trouble, necessary trouble."

For the rest of his life, John Lewis kept getting in good trouble. He was arrested something like forty-five times, including five times while he was in Congress. In 2009, at almost seventy, he was arrested by the Secret Service in a protest against the genocide in Darfur.

It would be wonderful if this kind of disruption didn't need to happen. If following the law and being on our best behavior was synonymous with doing the right thing. But that's just not how the world works. Certainly that's not how history has unfolded.

The pursuit of justice rarely involves respecting the status quo. How could it? If injustice exists, then by definition you must reject the status quo in order to address it. When Nietzsche described the philosopher's war against convention as one of knives, he was also describing perfectly the reality of the activist. It is a brutal fight, an up close and personal one. People will get hurt. Things will be cut to ribbons.

It means you throw yourselves into the spokes. Put yourself in front of the tanks. Be the squeaky wheel—the one who won't shut up, the one who repeats the truth that people don't want to hear.

Who do you do this for? You do it for the little guy. You do it for the people who can't do it for themselves. You do it for what is right.

"No woman has ever so comforted the distressed," Clare Boothe Luce said of Eleanor Roosevelt, "*or distressed the comfortable.*" Jesus and Gandhi are two men for whom the same could be said . . . and it should not surprise us that they had reputations as agitators too. Like Ashe, they had a choice to make. Did they hate injustice more than they loved decorum?

Yeah, we want and need allies . . . but we can't be paralyzed at the thought of creating enemies. Larry Kramer—an award-winning playwright and a gay rights activist who was relentless in raising awareness about the HIV/AIDS epidemic—didn't always get the balance right, notoriously alienating many of his friends.

But look, his job in that crisis was to wake people up, and the stakes were high. That required dispensing with some niceties.

"You're all going to be dead in five years. Every one of you fuckers," Larry Kramer told the gay community point-blank as AIDS began to ravage their ranks. "How about doing something about it? Why just line up for the cattle cars? Why don't you go out and make some fucking history?"

That's exactly what his group ACT UP did. Like the suffragettes, they disrupted public events and heckled politicians. They dumped the ashes of AIDS casualties on the White House lawn. They wrapped the home of a homophobic U.S. senator in a giant condom. They stormed the New York Stock Exchange and St. Patrick's Cathedral. They shut down the FDA in protest.

A couple of years later, disability activists used a similar playbook with their harrowing "Capitol Crawl," where they ditched their wheelchairs and crutches and crawled up the steps of the U.S. Capitol to demonstrate the barriers that they faced in daily life. How could lawmakers *not* respond?

This kind of publicity is a compelling form of communication, a way of forcing leaders and the public to see how the other half lives. It creates pressure, and the pressure leads to meetings and policy changes. And when authorities react poorly or worse, *overreact*—the ACT UP protestors were arrested countless times—it only further undermines their moral authority.

Good trouble does good work for good causes.

Sure, there are consequences to causing trouble. The jails that activists are thrown in—particularly the ones known to the suffragettes and the civil rights protestors—were not pleasant places. They were dangerous hellholes. Nor did all the activists live to be vindicated and recognized for their service, as Lewis and others did. But there is a stain to doing nothing too.

Larry Kramer saw something. He knew something. He refused to be silent about it. He insisted on *saying* something until people heard him. And had more doctors and administrators and politicians been willing to listen sooner, thousands of innocent people—including Arthur Ashe—would still be with us.

We need more people to cause more trouble.

Florence Nightingale caused plenty of good trouble, but where was her activism against war itself? Against colonialism itself? James Stockdale put incredible pressure on his captors, but given what he himself witnessed in the Gulf of Tonkin, what kind of pressure might he have applied on the Nixon administration for the final two years of the war after he returned home?

In the end, we are more likely to judge (and be judged) for trouble that *wasn't* caused than the trouble that was.

Don't just go along. Don't give the status quo more respect than it deserves.

Fight. Fight to help. Fight to make things better.

The goal is not to be liked. The goal is justice.

Like Arthur Ashe, the great Bill Russell chose to be difficult. Playing in an almost all-white game in the 1950s and '60s, he chose to ask questions. He staged protests. He chose confrontation. It wasn't always understood, it didn't always make a difference, but, as he said, it's "far better to accept the disputes of the world, the harassments, the arguments, the tensions, the slanders, the violence" than to ignore them. Than to be the tender turtle on the sidelines. "Men who ask have always succeeded," he said, "or been followed by men who have succeeded."

Which will you be?

What trouble will you seek?

What good trouble will you make?

Just Keep Going Back

~

Raphael Lemkin had spent the first half of the twentieth century trying to wake the world up to the terrible things people were doing to each other, first in Armenia and then in Europe.

No one listened.

So he backed up and decided to start very small. Part of the problem was that new technology had made violence possible at a scale difficult even to articulate. "As his armies advance," Churchill said of Hitler in 1941, "whole districts are exterminated. We are in the presence of a crime without a name."

Churchill almost always had the right words. Here, he did not.

That's what Lemkin solved for first.

Perhaps because the crime did not have a name, people made excuses, they made denials, they made false equivalences, they did nothing. In 1943, Lemkin changed history by coining the word "genocide" to describe the systematic, intentional destruction of a race of people. Just as Thomas Clarkson's powerful images of the slave trade irrevocably changed public perception, so too did this word—added to *Merriam-Webster*'s dictionary in 1950—change the moral arc of the universe.

There it was. It could not be denied.

After he introduced the word, he fought tirelessly to codify it into law—against inertia and incredible resistance. At Nuremberg, after the war he all but slept in the hallways as he advocated for a UN declaration against genocide. He hounded reporters for coverage. He mailed letters and research packages to politicians. He buttonholed diplomats. He wrote endless op-eds and articles. It was good trouble for a good cause.

It took more than four years, but finally, in 1948, the UN did it, topping their declaration with a unanimous treaty banning genocide—the nameless, awful thing that the Nazis were doing when they murdered Lemkin's mother.

All he could do was break down and weep.

Still, the fight was only beginning.

Even though the UN passed Lemkin's treaty, the United States refused to ratify it for decades. In 1967, a U.S. senator named William Proxmire picked up the baton. "The Senate's failure to act has become a national shame," he said. "I serve notice today that from now on I intend to speak day after day in this body to remind the Senate of our failure to act and of the necessity for prompt action."

This was not just virtue signaling either, because at that very moment, genocide was happening in Nigeria against the Christian Igbos. Within a few years, Pakistani troops would kill *mil-*

lions in Bangladesh. A genocide against the Hutu people in Burundi followed. And a genocide in Cambodia followed after that . . . and another followed after that.

Proxmire's speech was not successful. But he refused to accept the indifference. Instead, he addressed the Senate again and again and again until they heard him, giving some *three thousand* speeches to his fellow senators about genocide. He refused to be discouraged. He was relentless but also pragmatic, making countless trades and deals to slowly, steadily cajole the support of the sixty-seven senators he needed to ratify the treaty.

On October 1988, Proxmire rose to give his final speech about genocide, more than twenty years after his campaign began, forty years after Lemkin had begun. It was the 3,211th time he had done it across two decades. But now he could announce that the treaty had passed, that the world had a new tool to use in the fight to protect those most desperately in need of protection.

Of course, it would be wonderful if the world was naturally just, if people were automatically good, always doing the right thing. Sadly, they aren't and they don't. It's one of the most heartbreaking and frustrating things about life. Not only do people often not do the right thing, but they continue in error or evil even after they've been challenged, even after you've made every argument or followed all the procedures.

They dig in and they don't let go.

That was the Southern strategy during segregation. They held out, with racist officials hoping that if they could make things so difficult, so painful, so nasty, the North would give up, as they had after the Civil War with Reconstruction.

Which is why the civil rights movement was so much more than just marches. It was a series of endless court cases—cases that took years to get picked up, years to get their day in court, years to get the right verdict . . . and were then often ignored by Southern politicians and law enforcement officers. In the case of James Meredith, the black man who integrated the University of Mississippi, John Doar, a lawyer with the Justice Department, filed hundreds of motions, sat before multiple judges, appealed and appealed and appealed.

"You've just got to keep going back," Doar said of his legal strategy, whether it was dismantling segregation or prosecuting murderers. It didn't matter if the injunction went against them. It wasn't over just because a mayor or a governor ignored a ruling. It didn't matter if a mob besieged them, it didn't matter if no one was cooperating with their investigation. There was still time, there was still another motion, a new venue, an appeal, something they hadn't found yet.

The main thing was that the good guys didn't quit. That they didn't get discouraged. They had to continue to believe that they could—that they *would*—prevail.*

---

* It's hard not to see, looking at it now, how many of America's problems are rooted in the fact that Reconstruction ended early. John Doar had to keep going back because Northern politicians left in 1877.

Even after he was *shot in the head,* James Meredith kept at it. Doar didn't quit either. Just like Lemkin and Proxmire. Speech after speech. Motion after motion. Day after day. They stayed with it. They just kept going back, until finally, eventually, they made the tiniest bits of progress.

They did their job.

The Stoics say we build a life, create change, action by action, step by step. "No one can stop you from that," Marcus Aurelius wrote in *Meditations.* There's a fountain of goodness there, inside us, in the world, Marcus wrote. We must make sure it keeps bubbling up. No one can make you give up on your cause—that's the one thing you control. They can shower you with curses. They can erect countless obstacles. They can attack you with knives and fists (as happened to people like John Doar and James Meredith). They can bury you in paperwork. They can slow-walk you into near insanity.

But the decision to walk away? To quit on our business idea? To quit the organization? That's always ours.

We start small. We build allies. We look out for the little guy.

We have to act. We have to act, even if our impact is small, even if it is ignored, perhaps even if it feels like a suicide mission. Even if it seem like the impact will not be felt in our lifetime, we have to try.

Besides, if we can achieve our goals easily, if the changes come without resistance, are we really fighting the right battle? Defeats, setbacks, enemies? These are signs that we've aimed our sights high enough, that we're after something important, something that matters.

As we face them, we must keep going. We put one foot in front of the other. We follow the process, make the progress that we can.

We built momentum. We keep going back.

And eventually, inevitably, someone—we or someone carrying the torch we helped light—succeeds.

Then what?

We do what Proxmire said after he gave that final speech. We ignore the desire to celebrate. We refuse to rest on our laurels. We know that justice is never fully done.

We smile and we say, "I'm going to look around for something else."

Something Bigger Than Us . . .

~

> While Christ did not say to men, "Live for others," he
> pointed out that there was no difference at all between the
> lives of others and one's own life.
>
> —OSCAR WILDE

We are born perfectly selfish—caring only about our own needs, our own basic survival. Yet we are given at birth the model of perfect selflessness: the unconditional love of a parent.

All of us, it has been said, are here because someone took care of us when we were small and defenseless.

The work of our lives is to go from this dependence to dependability, from being taken care of to being a caretaker—but not just for our own children if we choose to have them, but for others, for ideas, for causes, for *justice* itself.

A Stoic named Hierocles famously illustrated this as a series of concentric circles. Each individual, he said, was born at the center of these circles, primarily concerned with ourself. With time, we expand our circles of concern or compassion to the people we love, the people who live around us, the people *like* us. But beyond these inner rings lies a larger world, composed of our fellow human beings spread out across the world, the environment, animals, even future generations we will never meet. The work of philosophy, he said, of *justice,* was the process of pulling these outer rings closer inward, caring about others as much as we care about ourselves.

The bigger our circles get, the bigger our heart gets, the better the world gets.

We have to realize that we are all part of one large family, each with a nature related to one another.

It was the "the most complete kind of madness," Hierocles wrote, "to wish to be joined with those who bear no affection toward us by nature and deliberately, to the greatest extent possible, to confer family bond on them."

But a beautiful madness, no?

The beauty of those who work tirelessly for a better future, who struggle and fight for the rights of others, who care about how the other half lives, who find a way to love their enemies, who find a way to do good in a world of evil . . . each blow against cruelty, each step forward for decency makes the next one more conceivable.

We have to care for those who cannot care for us—for those who do not care about us.

This is our responsibility.

This is our highest calling.

The work of our life.

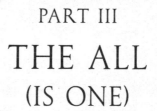

PART III
THE ALL
(IS ONE)

What made being alive almost worthwhile for me . . . was all the saints I met, who could be anywhere. By saints I meant people who behaved decently in a strikingly indecent society.

—KURT VONNEGUT

There is something beyond being a person of rectitude, something beyond being caring and compassionate—where goodness becomes a form of *greatness*. Each culture, each tradition has its own version of a saint. This is a person who does more than answer the call to courage and justice, but does so selflessly, with a poise and grace that seems almost superhuman. In them, it becomes something holy, something sacred. More than just embracing the "we"-ness of virtue, they embrace an expansive, radical connection to everyone and everything to ever live, expanding "we" to include everyone, to include all of us, even generations yet unborn. They care for more than just people and principles but for all things equally. They don't just do what's right but do it even when it costs them, even when, in some cases, it *costs them everything*. Are these men and women superhuman? No, they have been transformed, elevated by their commitment to righteousness in a way that we can similarly be transformed . . . if we so choose. If we so dedicate ourselves.

To So Love the World . . .

⌒

For a man of peace, it is remarkable how much of Gandhi's life was spent at war. Indeed, nearly the whole of it was spent pitted against one implacable foe after another—often violent and cruel ones. In every battle, Gandhi seemed to be almost impossibly mismatched, facing the most powerful forces on earth, be it the British Empire or the hardness of the human heart.

Yet each and every time, he emerged victorious—not only winning, but winning over his foes as well. Winning without any official office, without command of an army, without a fortune or income. He eschewed even basic technology, choosing instead, like the warriors of the most ancient of days, to fight wearing little more than sandals and a loincloth.

Albert Einstein, who so easily made sense of the most incomprehensible and complex of concepts, could only marvel at it. That one man could confront "brutality of Europe with the dignity of the simple human being" and despite every obstacle and temptation and struggle, rise superior at all times. "Generations to come," he said, "will scarcely believe that such a one as this even in flesh and blood walked upon this earth."

But he did. He very much did.

Mohandas Karamchand Gandhi was born in 1869 to an important family in Porbandar, India. A life of ease and provincial politics could have easily been his fate.

Yet something within him, like it did for Buddha, called him to go forth. Some god called him, some Krishna counseled this Arjuna away from an ordinary life toward the hero's journey, to something bigger, something beyond himself.

But to realize this destiny, to answer this call, Gandhi first had to conquer himself.

An early memory had an English teacher noticing that Gandhi had misspelled a word on a test. Hoping to preserve the class's perfect score—and advance his own career—the teacher motioned for Gandhi to copy off the classmate next to him. The temptation proffered. The temptation resisted. He preferred to fail than cheat and win. His reward? The teacher whom the student had so deeply admired walked off muttering of his pupil's "stupidity."

Gandhi was not born a saint—no one is. At age fifteen, Gandhi stole some money from his older brother. How much? For what? We don't really know, but as the days passed, he was steadily overcome with guilt. Confessing, he wrote a letter to his father in which he laid out his crimes and begged to be punished. His father, then dying of a fistula, sat up from his sickbed, read the letter from his son. Wordlessly, the man tore up the paper before collapsing. His boy broke down and wept, graced by the forgiveness of his father.

It would be one of their final encounters. Not long after, his father's health at its lowest ebb, Gandhi, then a married young man, asked to be relieved from his nursing duties by an uncle. Then he went to his bedroom and made love to his wife. While he was there, a terrible knock came at the door: His father had died.

He had missed saying goodbye to his father—for what, some transitory pleasure?—and it haunted him forever. Unable to give himself the grace that his father almost certainly would have given, Gandhi would lament years later that the "shame of my carnal desire at the critical moment of my father's death . . . is a blot I have never been able to efface or forget."

In every sense, this loss changed the course of Gandhi's life. In one sense it scarred him, in another it freed him. With little reason to stay in India and desperate to pursue new opportunities, it was decided by relatives that the young man should be sent to London to study law. His mother had only one condition. He must swear that while abroad he would not touch wine, women, or meat.

He gave his mother his word, and he would not break it, more or less for the rest of his monkish life.

As it happened, London was the genesis of his spiritual

awakening. It was actually there, almost five thousand miles from India, that Gandhi first read the Bhagavad Gita, one of the most sacred texts in Hinduism. It is the story of the warrior life, Krishna guiding Arjuna on the warrior's path. Gandhi was twenty when he read it for the first of many times. Every decision he made, close friends would later say, was a conscious attempt to live the message of the Gita. And then a chance encounter with a Bible salesman convinced Gandhi to spend some time with the seminal religious text of the West. While much of the Old Testament bored him, the Sermon on the Mount, which he would say "went straight to my heart," its message about turning the other cheek, delighted him beyond measure. He never converted to Christianity, of course, but he strove to be a living version of that sermon.

As a poor student, getting by on roughly a shilling a day, Gandhi learned by necessity what it meant to cut one's needs as close to nothing as possible. He also found that he didn't mind doing so, that he actually enjoyed the simple lifestyle that he'd later make famous.

In England, he took a public speaking class. He made decent marks in school. He joined a club for vegetarians. He made English friends. He met people of different religions. He met feminists and philosophers. He met doctors and socialists and Oxford scholars. In one exchange, Gandhi taught the Gita to two Englishmen and in return they taught him about Theosophy, an eclectic and strange grab bag of religious traditions.

In all the many generations of his family, none had ever left India—few had left home at all. Fewer still socialized outside their culture or caste. In England, Gandhi was exposed every single day to new people, new ideas, new cultures. As one of his British opponents would explain, were Gandhi's "ideas only of the East, he would have been content to have applied them to his personal existence in a life of meditative seclusion. It is only the teachings of the West that have made him an active social reformer." In fact, Gandhi's hunger for moral truth transcended this facile geographic distinction. He became a social reformer because he came to actually believe in these universal ideals of peace and equality and justice . . . *but the greatest of these is love.*

Two encounters stunned him, turned this small, half-hearted law student into the crusader who would change the world. The first happened in India, right after law school, when Gandhi's brother had gotten in some trouble with a British colonial official. Hoping to patch things up, Gandhi went to meet with the man. In London, he had been treated as a social equal. Here he was back in his home country, a trained lawyer, a member of an important local family, well within his rights and following official procedure. Yet what did it get him?

It got him physically manhandled by a colonizer.

Shortly afterward, while in South Africa trying a case, Gandhi was traveling by train to Pretoria. Boarding with a first-class ticket, he was asked to sit in third class because of his race. When he refused, he was removed with his bags from the train, spending a long, cold night alone by the tracks. The next day, traveling by stagecoach, he was blocked from sitting inside with the white passengers and then assaulted by the driver.

What was the point of this cruelty? Who did it serve?

Asked later to describe "the most creative experience of [his] life," Gandhi would point to that moment, the humiliation and the dehumanization of a legalized injustice. "The hardship to which I was subjected was superficial," he explained later, "only a symptom of the deep disease of color prejudice." It struck him at the train station, as it had Thomas Clarkson at the crossroads, that the evil could not be ignored, that he was just as qualified as anyone else to try "to root out the disease and suffer hardships in the process."

Shortly thereafter, news broke in South Africa of a bill that would deprive Indians of their voting rights, the first of many planned discriminatory policies aimed at the workers whom the British had imported to help build their colonies but now feared as a social and economic class. Gandhi had come to Natal to work on a few legal cases, always expecting to return home to Porbandar shortly after. The injustice of the of what he had experienced, that authorities were now attempting to codify into law, had shaken him. He expected to stay an extra month. The war would last for the next two decades.

In the early days of his activism, Gandhi started small. He represented indigent workers. He represented a Muslim who did not want to be forced, for religious reasons, to remove his cap in court. He published a few pamphlets arguing for equal rights for Indians. He founded a small newspaper. He wrote to British politicians in England. He founded the Natal Indian Congress, his first political organization. He cultivated allies and friends, including Henry Polak and Hermann Kallenbach, two Jewish men who would go on to serve and advise Gandhi for the rest of his life. He visited the slums, grasping for the first time how the other half lived, the indignities and injustices not just experienced daily by people in his community but inflicted by that community on their own members, the so-called untouchables.

All the while, he made a good and decent living as a hard-working lawyer—good enough that he went home to fetch his family and bring them to live with him in South Africa. It was on his return trip home that he experienced a third and clarifying brush with racial hatred, this one far more dangerous than the others. As he sat in his boat off the coast of Africa with a few hundred other Indians, a vicious rumor spread that he and his fellow passengers were part of an invasion of illegal immigrants, a convoy of diseased and parasitic newcomers who would overwhelm and replace the current ruling class. It was the great replacement theory. It was viral misinformation. Jim Crow and the KKK. An old song, sung, as it seems to be, forever.

"It is the intention of these facile and delicate creatures to make themselves proprietors of the only thing that the rulers of this country had withheld from them—the franchise," one speaker said to an angry mob who gathered at the shore. "It was their intention to put themselves in parliament and legislate for the Europeans; to take over the household management, and put the Europeans in the kitchen."

Gandhi was told it might be safer for him to disembark under the cover of night. Finding nothing in nonviolence that obligated him to be a coward, he refused. A mob met him, and he met the mob, enduring their blows and whips, coming within seconds of being lynched—a crowd chanting that they would string him up "on a sour apple tree."

"Gandhi *ought* to have hated every white face to the end of his life," the Oxford scholar and friend of Gandhi's, Edward Thompson, observed. The incident on the shore hardened Gandhi only in one sense—the mob he forgave, but the cause, the cause he would now see through to the end. And he would do so by making his followers better, not by indulging their worst.

Because Gandhi is so well-known for his campaigns in India, his work in South Africa is largely forgotten. As it happens, it was during his time in South Africa, protecting the rights of Hindu and Muslim immigrants from the early outcroppings of the racial hatred that would kill millions over the next century, that not only his reputation but a great breakthrough in human affairs were made.

In the early 1900s, Gandhi went to London on several occasions to lobby the colonial offices for better treatment of his people—to demand their rights as British subjects. It was there that he witnessed the work of the suffragettes, their movement just then accelerating. He would attend one of their meetings, speaking with Emmeline Pankhurst herself.

"Today the whole country is laughing at them," he would write back in South Africa, "and they have only a few people on their side. But undaunted, these women work steadfast in their cause. They are bound to succeed and gain the franchise, for the simple reason that deeds are better than words."

On January 11, 1908, back in South Africa, defying a law that required every male "Asiatic" to submit fingerprints, undergo physical examinations, and carry a registration certificate at all times, Gandhi found himself in the same court where as a lawyer he had tried so many times to keep his clients out of jail. Now he was asking the judge to give him the full sentence under the law. Within days, hundreds of supporters would join him there.

The Indians had been discriminated against because they were thought to be lesser people, a politically powerless, hopelessly divided group—Hindu, Muslim, rich, poor, free, indentured. Yet here they were, a coordinated wave of men—and later women—one right after another, in silent and unstoppable defiance of the law.

He had commanded that they "fill the jails" . . . and they did!

"Gandhi," one of his closest political allies would explain, "has in him the marvelous spiritual power to turn ordinary men around him into heroes and martyrs."

"When I first launched out on Satyagraha," Gandhi explained, "I had no companion. We were 13,000 men, women, and children against a whole nation capable of crushing this existence out of us. I did not know who would listen to me. It all came as in a flash. All the 13,000 did not fight back. Many fell back. But the honor of the nation was saved. New history was written by the South African *satyagraha*."

That word—*satyagraha*—is the most important word in that new history, perhaps one of the most important words in the history of the human race.* "Passive resistance" was a term of some popularity at the time, pioneered by the suffragettes, but Gandhi felt it woefully insufficient. Because what he was doing wasn't passive, it was *active*. It sought out conflict, not violent conflict, but conflict between justice and injustice, where justice would have the opportunity to prove its superiority in all ways, where injustice would be forced into the open, all its contradictions and cruelties exposed.

There, in this critical moment, the "victim" could, through patience and courage, demonstrate their humanity, their dignity, their grace to an oppressor or an indifferent public who did not think they had any. Would *satyagraha* always win or achieve its political aims? Perhaps not, Gandhi readily accepted, but it

---

* Gandhi's cousin came up with *sadagraha,* a word that means "firmness in good cause," which Gandhi tweaked to *satyagraha*: firmness in truth or love force.

would never fail in the process to prove its own goodness. It would help the practitioner reach a higher spiritual plane.

"The grandest aid to development of strong, pure, beautiful character which is our aim, is the endurance of suffering," Gandhi said in a 1909 speech. "Self-restraint, unselfishness, patience, gentleness, these are the flowers which spring beneath the feet of those who accept, but refuse to impose suffering, and the grim prisons of Johannesburg, Pretoria, Heidelberg, and Volkrust are like the four gateways to this garden of God."

During his first stint in jail, Gandhi read Thoreau's *Civil Disobedience*. Thoreau, who had read the Gita and other Indian texts, had gone to jail in protest of the expansion of slavery. In South Africa, Gandhi had also fallen in love with writings of Leo Tolstoy, not the novels but his Christian works that preached nonviolence and compassion, that the kingdom of God was in each individual person.

Tolstoy and Thoreau. Emmeline Pankhurst. The Sermon on the Mount. The Bhagavad Gita. The Koran. All of it came together. Pierre Teilhard de Chardin, a French philosopher who, like Gandhi, would serve bravely as a stretcher-bearer in war, explained that those who remain true to themselves, who move toward consciousness and love, eventually find themselves united at a summit with "all those who, from every direction, have made the same ascent. For everything that rises must converge."

The idea, the way was always there, but it converged in Gandhi at a moment in time that changed everything.

Before Gandhi, what was the remedy of those who disagreed with the government? Violence. By what means could a person strike back against tyranny? Violence. And how was the government to respond to these threats? With violence. Both sides proving to each other their inhumanity. It was an inescapable circle of escalating brutality, despair, and hopelessness that brought the worst out of everyone, that inevitably, as Gandhi would later famously say, made the whole world blind.*

Gandhi had seen war up close, caring for the wounded in the Boer War. He had seen the horrors of what people were willing to do to each other. Believing there was another way, he would put his body on the line to prove it. "Gandhi resisted evil with as much vigor and power as a violent resistor," Martin Luther King Jr. would later observe, "but he resisted with love instead of hate. True pacifism is not unrealistic submission to evil power. It is rather a courageous confrontation of evil by the power of love."

Both men would brilliantly—one could also say poetically—use the religion of their oppressors against them, taking the ideals that had been given to them by those oppressors and turning them into both a shield and a sword. Yet equally brilliant was the way that both men, especially Gandhi in his early years, combined saintlike idealism with an earthly pragmatism. As a

---

* Contrast Gandhi's legacy with the revolutions that followed the "innovations" of Marx and Lenin . . . from which we could conservatively estimate more than a hundred million people have died.

lawyer in South Africa, Gandhi had fought for the right of a Muslim to be able to wear his cap in court. But this was the same Gandhi who, in order to be accepted to the bar, had willingly removed the headdress of his faith, reserving his strength, he said, "for fighting bigger battles."

Almost immediately after going to jail for the first time, Gandhi agreed to a compromise with the political powers in South Africa. In exchange for a promise to lift the most onerous legal obligations against Indians, Gandhi agreed to voluntarily submit to the same registration requirements he had just resisted. He would not accept legalized inferiority—because once it began, once it was in the legal record, where would it end? Some of his supporters were upset, but he argued it was the best deal they could get. In fact, that's what he consistently sought throughout his career, deals that made things better, even if only a tiny bit so. Gandhi was an idealist, a purist . . . he was also an incrementalist.

It was always a virtuous kind of pragmatism, but a pragmatism nevertheless. Most important, it was an effective kind that got things done. "Inside the saint or near-saint," George Orwell would write of Gandhi, "there was a very shrewd and able person."

This was a man who could have done anything. His legal career had flourished in South Africa, affording him an enormous income and a house on the beach. But he gave all that up, choosing to live communally on an ashram, putting more and more hours into the cause until there were not enough hours in the day to practice law. Although he fought for the rights of Indians to travel as they pleased, he himself traveled third class by choice, wishing to experience the same hardships as not just Indians but all poor people in the country. He gave up sex. His ambitions evolved personal concerns to something close to selflessness, refusing at one point some jewels that had been offered to him in gratitude by his supporters, even as his wife begged that he accept them for his children's future. No, Gandhi insisted that they be given to the Natal Indian Congress to start an emergency fund.

Like Truman, Gandhi also possessed the wonderful ability to change. For most of his time in South Africa, as he fought against the injustices of the colonial offices, it only belatedly occurred to him that he himself was a colonizer. He used racist terms to refer to the native Africans, referring them as "savages" and worse. He did not originally seem to be particularly concerned with their rights, in fact, he was aghast that the British would legally lump Indians in with the natives.

It was his time as a stretcher-bearer that opened his eyes. "I shall never forget," he said years later, "the lacerated backs of the Zulus who had received stripes and were brought to us for nursing because no white nurse was prepared to look after them." The hypocrisy of the Christians who had inflicted these punishments struck him as disgusting—but it also prompted him to evaluate his own hypocrisies. Education or wealth didn't make someone superior, he understood, *it was how they treated the most vulnerable.* The Gandhi that would emerge in India, the destroyer of caste and untouchability, was born there, as he examined his own faults.

More than five decades before Martin Luther King Jr. spoke of his dream in Washington, Gandhi spoke of the same idea but as *an obligation.* "If we look to the future," he told an audience in Johannesburg in 1908, "is it not a heritage to have to leave to posterity, that all the different races commingle and produce a civilization that perhaps the world has not yet seen?" That's what he fought for there in Natal, repeatedly defying the law, turning himself not just into a growing global figure but a savvy political organizer in the process.

By 1914, Gandhi's work in South Africa was done, having reached what he felt was an acceptable compromise with the South African government to protect the rights of minorities. "The saint has left our shores," his longtime adversary General Jan Smuts said with relief, "I sincerely hope forever."

Gandhi was forty-four years old. He could have considered retirement or returned to his legal practice, resting satisfied with his contribution to public life. Instead, he was boarding a ship back to India, where his next battles awaited. "I shall, of course, continue to work for you," he told the Indians he was leaving behind. "You are under indenture for one person for five years, but I am under indenture with 300 millions [all of India] for a life-time. I shall go on with that service and never displace you from my heart." In all, Gandhi spent 250 days in jail in South Africa. It was not a prelude of what was to come but a down payment.

As a young man, Gandhi had gone to England and left with a law degree. He had gone to South Africa to become a lawyer and left an activist. Mohandas returned to India as *the Mahatma*—the great-souled one.

He would spend the next year in India with his ears open and his mouth shut. India was then a country of enormous poverty and suffering. Hundreds of thousands died each year from tuberculosis. Millions were infected with malaria. Famine was common. Her resources had been plundered by the British, who ruled her as a colonial power—just a few hundred thousand British ruling over hundreds of millions of Indians— deliberately dividing the people against themselves, exploiting and abusing them. Gandhi knew that he would lead India to her destiny, free her from the injustice that had ruled over her for nearly two hundred years, but how? When? He would wait for a sign.

In the meantime, change began—as it always does—with self-reformation.

Any freedom from the British, he said, "is a meaningless term if we desire to keep a fifth of India under perpetual subjection," speaking of "untouchability"—an ancient and degrading form of caste oppression that condemned millions of Hindus to an almost subhuman status, preventing them from entering temples and subjecting them to random violence.*

In 1915, he stunned his nascent movement by inviting an untouchable to come live with him and his family in their ashram, later adopting one as his own daughter. When a patron pulled his funding in response, Gandhi shrugged, saying he'd happily live in the slums with the untouchables—whom he had come to know and admire for their bravery in South Africa—if it came to that. "My conscience tells me that untouchability can never be a part of Hinduism," he said. "I do not think it too much to dedicate my whole life to removing the thick crust of sin with which Hindu society has covered itself for so long by stupidly regarding these people as untouchables. I am only sorry that I am unable to devote myself wholly to that work."

The reason he could not do that is that he got a call from mill workers in Ahmedabad.

Once again, the dispute was not yet against the British. Instead, workers simply wanted better wages from the mill owners, most of whom were Indian. Gandhi sided instinctively with the underdog, even though one of the mill owners had person-

---

* Gandhi began later to refer to the untouchables as *harijans*—children of god—saying, "Not that the change of name brings about any change of status but one may at least be spared the use of a term which is itself one of reproach."

ally funded his ashram when it had been abandoned over his support of untouchables. Three weeks into a strike, the will of the workers collapsed. "What is it to Gandhi?" they asked when he tried to encourage them. "You come and go in your car . . . eat sumptuous food, but we are suffering death-agonies; attending meetings does not prevent starvation."

In response, Gandhi announced on March 15, 1918, that he would go on a hunger strike in solidarity with the workers. He had fasted before in pursuit of spiritual purification, he had done it to settle disputes in his ashram, but he had little sense of its political power. In fact, it had been intended as a gesture to encourage the workers, to demonstrate his fidelity, yet by accident, he also applied painful pressure to the mill owners. Three days later, both sides agreed to arbitration—arbitration that eventually awarded a 35 percent raise to the workers.

Satyagraha now had another incredibly powerful weapon.

Soon after, Gandhi began to advocate for what he called a *hartal*—a full strike against the British occupation of India. The idea of noncooperation became key to his vision of a free India. How could they continue to cooperate with their oppressors? How would they claim to be worthy of freedom from something they were so obviously dependent on? Whose trains they used, whose taxes they paid, whose liquor they drank, whose goods they coveted, whose style of dress they mimicked, whose schools they attended. The prize wasn't freedom, but what he called *swaraj,* or self-rule. To become independent in law, they must first become independent *in fact*—by breaking free mentally, spiritually, ethically.

Independence then was not just an end but a *means.*

Nothing captured this better than Gandhi's famous Salt March, a twenty-four-day walk across India in protest of Britain's monopoly on salt. The world followed breathlessly as this small man defied an empire, taking his pinch of salt and motioning the people to follow him, to fill up the jails once again. More than sixty thousand arrests followed in his wake—men and women were beaten mercilessly, heads cracked by rifle butts, fingers stomped under bootheels, as the people sought the most basic use of their own country's natural resources. In a single exchange, all pretense of British authority collapsed—all that was left was power . . . power that eroded by the day under his unrelenting protests.

India was free. Like Frederick Douglass deciding he would no longer be whipped—that he'd die before he'd let an overseer touch him—it would take years for the legal niceties of home rule to get worked out, but they now had the upper hand.

With a word, Gandhi could have lit the country on fire. Riots. Sabotage. Assassinations. All-out war. India was at his disposal, waiting on his command. This was a man so beloved that he was literally rubbed raw by admirers as he walked, requiring a kind of Vaseline bath each night just to keep campaigning. He had weapons that would have brought pressure faster.

Yet he never used them. For more than thirty years, Gandhi remained strictly nonviolent, even as the British brutalized, even massacred his supporters. He knew that to respond would only escalate the conflict; it would irrevocably change him and his country's character. So he patiently, heartbreakingly endured suffering, fighting . . .

Victory was inevitable, he believed. What mattered right now, in every moment, was that they did the right thing.

As he addressed enormous crowds, Gandhi would hold up the five fingers of his hand, one by one. "This is equality for untouchables," he would say. Another was for equality for women. A third was for Hindu and Muslim cooperation. Another was sobriety—from wine and opium and other urges. A fifth was for spinning—that is, economic self-sufficiency. What bound these fingers to the body was the wrist, which he said was for nonviolence.

"No matter what you do," Gandhi told the British, "no matter how you repress us, we shall one day wring reluctant repentance from you; and we ask you to think betimes, and take care what you are doing, and see that you do not make the three hundred millions of India your eternal enemies."

Did they listen? Of course not.

Over and over again he was arrested. Over and over again people were beaten and trampled upon.

It didn't work. It couldn't.

The power of a machine gun is muted against people who do

not fear death. The power of the dollar doesn't work against people who prize only what is free and naturally theirs. "Be careful in dealing with a man who cares nothing for sensual pleasures, nothing for comfort or praise or promotion, but is simply determined to do what he believed to be right," a British scholar had warned of Gandhi. "He is a dangerous and uncomfortable enemy because his body which you can always conquer gives you so little purchase of his soul."

At the time and since, people questioned Gandhi's methods in light of the barbarity of the twentieth century. How does a hunger strike stop a tank? What hope does *satyagraha* have when the enemy sends its prisoners to gas chambers? Gandhi was not glib when he suggested nonviolence was always the answer, though his ignorance of modern technology probably limited his understanding of what humans were capable of doing to each other.

In a famous essay titled "If I Were a Czech," Gandhi argued that massive civilian resistance to tyranny and genocide could work—not only because it would destroy a tyrant's authority but because it would engender international sympathy. Hitler was a brutal murderer, intent on killing as many Jews as possible. Gandhi believed that if this violence had been forced out into the open, as the Indians had done with the British, his reign would have been shorter and international support may have come faster. "Its real quality is only tested in such cases," he said of nonviolence during the war. "Sufferers need not see the result during their lifetime. They must have faith that if their cult survives, the result is a certainty. The method of violence gives no greater guarantee than that of non-violence."

It's perfectly reasonable to disagree with Gandhi here. He himself saw the moral issue for what it was, saw the tragedy for what it was. "Even after he had completely adjured violence," Orwell wrote of Gandhi, "he was honest enough to see that in war it is usually necessary to take sides."

What's indisputable is that nonviolence worked in India and it transformed Gandhi. Having discarded want and desire, having triumphed over his fear of death, having given himself over completely to a selfless cause, he was perfectly fearless. "Thank you," a smiling Gandhi said as he met with the British viceroy, the man who had clapped him in jail many times, the man with the power to execute him. Then he reached into the folds of his linen shawl and pulled out the fruits of his illegal march. "I will put some of this salt into my tea," he said mischievously, "to remind us of the famous Boston Tea Party."

He had become "untouchable" in a different sense, above, beyond, higher than the physical realm. And by extension, so had the millions of poor, suffering people who had chosen this man not as their elected leader but as their spiritual model.

Meanwhile, Gandhi insisted on listening to the British, trying to understand them, trying to appeal to something decent inside them. "Three fourths of the miseries and misunderstandings in the world will disappear," he explained to his followers, "if we step into the shoes of our adversaries and understand their standpoint."

Gandhi worked tirelessly to treat his opponents well. Once, before a surgery by a British doctor, Gandhi called the medical team in to draft a public statement thanking them in advance for their treatment and absolving them in advance if anything went wrong. His greatest fear was that his own supporters would be violent, and he had no hesitation about canceling any event he believed might devolve into rioting.

He was also just plain considerate, once calling off a protest because the British were dealing with a railway strike. He paused a campaign over Christmas and New Year's so his Christian opponents could spend time with their families. He postponed a campaign that would have landed on Easter Sunday. He paused campaigns multiple times during both world wars, empathizing with all that England had on its plate . . . even as her boot was on his neck.

Before each and every campaign, he explained to his opponents exactly what he was going to do and where—giving them one final chance to think better of it. He never lost his preference for negotiation and face-to-face meetings, hoping for the best from each viceroy that the British rotated in to beat him. "I have always to see those who have opposed me," he said, "so that I can explain my position." It rarely worked. "An Englishman will not be argued into yielding," Gandhi once wrote to his son, "he yields only under the compulsion of events." Yet he kept arguing, kept appealing to the better angels of their nature, kept insisting on the better angels of his own nature, even as he accumulated more and more power. Why? Because it made him, his followers, and the British better. "Men say I am a saint losing myself in politics," he once joked. "The fact is that I am politician trying my hardest to be a saint."

Meanwhile, Churchill couldn't even stomach the idea of negotiating with Gandhi, finding it "alarming and nauseating to see Mr. Gandhi, a seditious Middle Temple lawyer, now posing as a fakir of a type well-known in the east, striding half naked up the steps of the viceregal palace, while he is still organizing and conducting a campaign of civil disobedience, to parley on equal terms with the representative of the Emperor-King." He was right in the sense that Gandhi was not an equal—through the cleansing and elevating power of *satyagraha,* he had made himself in every way the superior.

Using Christian ideals of the West against the Westerners and the ideals of Hinduism and Islam to rally his own supporters, Gandhi was able to force both to stare their own shortcomings in the face. Nor was he simply talking about these ideals, he *embodied* them, living on next to nothing, suffering voluntarily, trusting endlessly, forgiving constantly, calling on *all* to do better. None of his opponents—Indian or British—could deny that they admired him.

It's why his hunger strikes, which he underwent eighteen times over the course of thirty-four years, were so effective. No one wanted to be responsible for letting him down, let alone killing him. Nowhere was this clearer than in General Smuts—whom Gandhi had fought with in South Africa, now one of Gandhi's allies—regularly writing the British government not to imprison the man but to negotiate with him in good faith, and at one point writing to Gandhi to try and talk him out of a potentially fatal twenty-one-day fast.

He had destroyed his foe by turning him into a friend.

As the twentieth century went on, Gandhi, like Truman, found himself entrusted with enormous power. Would his fundamental decency hold up under the strain of the world's stage? There was no tyranny. No score settling. There was no corruption. No malice. No ambition. No bad faith. No difference between the public and private figure. If you were dictator of India for a day, he was once asked, what would you do? "I would not accept it," he said simply. *Yes, but if you had to.* I would clean the houses of the untouchables, Gandhi said, and convert my official residence into a hospital. And if given a second day in charge, he said he'd continue in that vein.

For all the trials and ordeals, the insane tests of will and human suffering—more than twenty-three hundred days in jail, decades as a political fighter—he never cracked, never betrayed his own message, took shortcuts, gave in to fear, or accepted favors. "Compared with other leading political figures of our time," Orwell would write after Gandhi's death, "how clean a smell he had managed to leave behind."

Just the same simple message on repeat, patiently, lovingly rendered. "When we are tired of breaking each other's heads," he said, "we shall discover that, despite the disparities of our races and religions, we can live together."

In the end, it wasn't the British who most challenged his faith in that noble—some said hopelessly naive—idea. In 1947, the British left. It happened slowly . . . then all at once. The external enemy that had bound Indians of many faiths and castes together was gone. He had driven the conquerors away without firing a shot, one man defeating the empire that even Hitler and Stalin combined could not break.

But the victory was bittersweet, because the British had left and taken with them any chance of a united India. The country was split. A great migration, a great conflagration of Hindus and Muslims commenced, one of tragic, unimaginable violence. Millions died as India was partitioned.

Gandhi was seventy-eight years old, but he headed straight for the worst of it. "All I know is that I won't be at peace with myself unless I go there," he said on his journey to Calcutta. He insisted, begged for peace between the two religions, and when it didn't come, he put his body on the line one final time.

"I therefore begin fasting from 8:15 tonight to end only if and when sanity returns to Calcutta," he announced, staying with a Muslim family in a Muslim area to make a point about tolerance. It was a potentially intractable, irresolvable conflict—thousands of years of religious differences—but he was not intimidated.

"Somehow we never think of a Gandhi fast as a terrible experience," one writer observed. "We think of it as a political maneuver, a strike, a gesture. But here it was in human terms, a process."* Gandhi, now very old, would kill himself—slowly, excruciatingly—before he would assent to violence. He would give his last breath if it could save one soul.

"In Punjab we have 55 thousand soldiers and large scale rioting on our hands," Britain's final viceroy, Lord Mountbatten, would write back to England. "In Bengal our force consists of one man and there is no rioting." As Hindus and Muslims rushed to him to surrender their weapons, Gandhi gave a warning they did not doubt. "If the peace is broken again," he said, "I will come back and undertake a fast unto death and die if necessary."

It was perhaps an impossible hope, or at least an impossible one in so short a span. In any case, Gandhi would not live long enough to return. Once again, though not by choice, an opponent would choose to use violence against him.

"I am not acting for martyrdom," he had said many years earlier, "but if it comes in my way . . . I shall have well earned it,

---

*In one twenty-one-day hunger strike in 1943, Gandhi lost 20 percent of his body weight . . . in his seventies.

and it will be possible for the historian of the future to say that the vow I had taken before Harijans that I would, if need be, die in the attempt to remove untouchability was literally fulfilled."

In October 1947, as he said goodbye to his grandson, he handed him a small slip of paper that listed the seven blunders of humanity.

Wealth without work.
Pleasure without conscience.
Knowledge without character.
Commerce without morality.
Science without humanity.
Religion without sacrifice.
Politics without principle.

The work of his life, he said, had been to address these root causes of injustice and the violence that followed them. And it was this legacy that he hoped his family and his followers would continue.

In the afternoon of January 30, 1948, on his way to a multi-faith prayer gathering, Gandhi walked down the garden of Birla House. Shots rang out. An assassin—a Hindu nationalist who found Gandhi too accommodating of Muslim demands—fired three bullets into the mahatma at point-blank range. Gandhi's last words were "He! Rama." *Oh! God.*

Again, he seems to have known it would always end this way.

"Death is the appointed end of all life. To die by the hand of a brother, rather than by disease or in some such other way, cannot be for me a matter of sorrow," he had prophesied long before. "I am free from the thought of anger or hatred against my assailant," he said. "I know that that will redound to my eternal welfare, and even the assailant will later on realize my perfect innocence."

If he'd had the chance, he would have loved more than anything to forgive the man who had shot him, he'd have smiled as his hero in the Gita had, blessing him and everyone he'd ever struggled with before he left this world. And if Gandhi had any say over who he came back as in the next life, we know for a fact that he would have chosen to come back as one of the untouchables for whom he had fought so hard.

Gandhi's body was burned on a funeral pyre the next day. He had not wanted a funeral or a monument. His legacy was there in his deeds, it was to live on in his spirit, to be turned into a legacy by the people who carried it forward.

"The light has gone out of our lives and there is darkness everywhere," his chosen successor, Jawaharlal Nehru, said in his famous eulogy. "The light has gone out, I said, and yet I was wrong. For the light that shone in this country was no ordinary light. The light that has illuminated this country for these many years will illuminate this country for many more years, and a thousand years later that light will still be seen in this country and the world will see it and it will give solace to innumerable hearts. For that light represented . . . the living, eternal truths."

And now, that small light in a dark room provides hope for us. We can choose to branch off from Gandhi's coaching tree, to pick up his mantle to create a better world through . . .

. . . self-sacrifice and suffering

. . . high standards of personal conduct

. . . friendship and tolerance

. . . lifting up the unfortunate and vulnerable

. . . virtuous pragmatism

. . . the transformative power of nonviolence

. . . forgiveness and love

. . . and more love and more love and more love.

It will be a long journey. It will be a fight whose victory we may not live to see.

But the more we give to it, the more we'll get out of it.

Climb Your Second Mountain

~

The first thirty-five years of Lou Gehrig's life were defined by a monastic discipline. Baseball wasn't just everything, it was the only thing. He was a slave to the game, he said, but the result of all this was a form of greatness whose purity one sees but once in a generation, perhaps once in the history of the game.

He could hit anything. Endure everything. Do anything that winning required.

And he did. Six times a World Series champion, 2,130 consecutive games. He was a multitime All-Star, a multitime MVP. He won the Triple Crown. He hit almost 500 home runs.

He brought people joy and happiness through his work, he made his teammates and the game better by being in it. To say he reached his potential is an absurd understatement.

But then it all came crashing down. Amyotrophic lateral sclerosis (ALS) stripped him of his ability to run and to catch. His career was cut short. His glory days with the Yankees ended forever.

We know from Gehrig's famous "luckiest man in the world" speech that he didn't pity himself, that he didn't whine about what was stolen from him, that he took the sentence that fate had in store for him with dignity and poise and fearlessness.

But how many people know what he did next?

Although Gehrig could have spent the final—and tragically few—remaining years of his life relaxing comfortably with the savings he diligently stockpiled, he didn't. Instead, he took another job.

Like Truman after office, he was offered everything: $30,000 to lend his name to a restaurant, $40,000 to appear regularly at a nightclub. All these he turned down to take a government job as the head of New York City's parole board. It paid just $5,700 a year and meant long hours in dank prisons and stuffy offices, but he took it.

Gehrig's biographer would write that "with his doom sealed and his parting from the woman [his wife] who have given him the only real happiness he had ever known, inevitable, he chose to spend his last days, not in one final feverish attempt to suck from life in two years all that he might have had in forty, but in work and service ... [giving] unstintingly of what strength there was left to him."

Even as his health failed, he drove each day to the office, pored over paperwork, rendered the impossibly difficult decisions, to which he had to affix a rubber stamp, unable as he was to physically sign his own name.* Theodore Roosevelt, speaking of a different sport but nailing Gehrig's transition almost perfectly, once said, "It is a good thing to be a good half-back but it is a mighty bad thing if at forty all you can say of a man is that he was a good half-back." There in his midthirties, the game he had loved gone, Gehrig found a way to be great in a profoundly different way, giving back to the city and to the people from which he himself had gotten so much.

The writer David Brooks would famously call this "the Second Mountain." We get to the top of the first mountain of our lives, he explained, conquering business or sports or some artistic domain. It's wonderful. It's rewarding—financially most of all. It may well do good for others and the world. Yet in the recesses of our mind, we feel there is something anticlimactic about this success. We survey our kingdom and find ourselves wondering . . .

Is this all there is?

Maybe we get a diagnosis like Gehrig. Or we have an accident. Or we fall into a deep depression. Or someone tells us something, gives us a peek into how the rest of the world is, how the other half lives.

Life is telling us something. The emptiness is a sign.

---

* One such case was the future middleweight champion Rocky Graziano, whom Gehrig sent back to reform school.

Will we just go back to how we've always done things? Or will we find another mountain, one that is much higher, much less a monument to our ego? One that challenges us to reach our potential in a fuller sense, a less self-interested way, a more generous and community-minded way.

There was the time for us to earn, earn, earn, and then later, it's a time to give, give, give, to help, help, help.

Sammy Davis Jr. spent years "thinking about nothing but *making* it," and then once he had made it, about nothing but enjoying it. But then? But then what? "There comes a time when [a person] wants something else, something *more*," he said, because money and fame and fun were "not enough to justify your life." So he threw himself into civil rights, threw himself into helping the less fortunate. Decades later, another great singer, David Lee Roth, would find himself at a similar crossroads and decide to become a paramedic in New York City.

It doesn't matter what the second mountain is. It just has to be about something beyond your own well-being.

Barack Obama, speaking with the author Doris Kearns Goodwin, once talked about how "common" ambition is in most of us when we're young. We want to get rich. We want to make our father proud of us. We want to make a mark on the world. But as we get older, he said, this ambition has to burn away, especially if we are fortunate enough to have done any of that, in our own way. In its place something broader, something deeper should appear—in his case, he explained, his north star became "creating a world in which people of different races or backgrounds or faiths can recognize each other's humanity, or creating a world in which every kid, regardless of their background, can strive and achieve and fulfill their potential."

But what about you? It can't be *another* VC exit. *Another* winning season. *Another* big client.

Seriously, who cares?! Not only have you already done this . . . so have countless other people.

It's time to follow our north star to the next peak, the next challenge—one that is more spiritual than material, that makes us *and others* better by taking it on.

Not another challenge; we've had plenty of those, not like a musician trying their hand at acting, but more like an investment banker getting their certification and becoming an elementary school teacher. A mountain that is less about you, less about stuff, less about beating or crushing or extracting and far more about almost everyone, more about *all of us.*

Stop Asking for the Third Thing

⌒

What the writer Dawn Dorland did was incredible. She gave her kidney to a stranger. By literally opening up her body and giving away a piece of herself, she saved someone's life. Even more beautifully, her donation inspired the spouse of the recipient (who was not a match) to give their own kidney to someone else.

What an angel.

Most people who knew her one saw her that way.

Except one.

As Dorland began to post about her donation and the recovery process, her friends were supportive. But as nice as they were, what stuck out to Dorland was that one of them, an acquaintance and fellow writer named Sonya Larson, was oddly silent. And so in a moment that they both would rue forever, she wrote the woman to ask why.

What would ensue was a tragic, almost comic conflict whose escalation even the most imaginative novelist could not have predicted. Dorland's very human desire for recognition, to be appreciated for what she did, Larson's cynicism and sensitivity, the social faux pas, the fragile egos, the whims of the creative process, and the power of social media would collide first in a fictional and unflattering short story Larson wrote about a woman with a "white-savior" complex, and would culminate in lawsuits, accusations of plagiarism, and a flood of publicity.

The nicest thing that Dorland had ever done was turned into a farce, portrayed as an act of narcissism or worse. Larson in turn spent thousands and thousands of dollars she didn't have to defend her art in court from Dorland, whose thin-skinnedness and need for attention all but proved the caricature Larson had portrayed in her fiction.

None of it should have happened—none of it except the original sin, or rather, the original kindness.

But this is what the ancients would have told us, that nothing good results from trying to chase down gratitude or recognition for what you've done. "When you've done well and another has benefited by it, why like a fool do you look for a third thing on top—credit for the good deed or a favor in return?" Marcus Aurelius would ask himself.

And repeatedly Marcus would return to this idea in *Meditations,* because like the rest of us, he was frustrated when his best efforts weren't always understood or appreciated, let alone repaid. In fact, that was the fate of a leader, he later joked—to earn a bad reputation while doing good things.

It's long been said that being a good person is a thankless

task . . . but if you're doing it for the thanks, how good are you really?

It's not just that chasing the third thing will get us into trouble, as it did for Dorland, but that it undermines what we've done. In a sense, both of her acts are incomprehensible. Writing to a friend to say, in effect, why haven't you acknowledged this incredible thing I've done? So extra. Giving up a vital organ for someone she'd never met? *Also extra!* And yet the former tarnishes the beauty of the latter.

When Churchill called America's rescue of Europe after World War II the "most unsordid act in history," he must have in part been referring to Truman's waving off of recognition or legacy. "I'm not doing this for credit," Truman would explain. "I am doing it because it's right. I am doing it because it's necessary to be done if we're to survive ourselves."

But the thanklessness of it, the selflessness of it, that was what made it great. That was also what made it so strategically brilliant. Certainly, the Soviets could never have done it themselves—and, in fact, the offer itself, which was extended to the Soviet Bloc, was baffling to them.

So Truman spent all his political capital to give capital away, to a largely underwhelming reaction at the time. But he had been there before. For decades, his politically clean hands had been unrecognized. In fact, he was unfairly given a reputation for being corrupt! It was not right . . . but then again, neither would the alternative have been. Should Truman have taken the bribes because, *what the hell, everyone already thinks I am corrupt anyway*?

Better to do right and go unrewarded than to do wrong and go unpunished.

Besides, the doing is a reward. Feel amazing for doing an amazing thing—you don't need anyone to *tell* you that you are.

The Bible reminds us in Matthew 6:2 not to sound the trumpets announcing what you've done. Jesus also reminded his followers that when one looks back behind them when plowing, they allow the horses to drift. So it goes when we look back and admire what we've done, relishing our specialness or generosity. It's a distraction from moving forward, it's a lapse in judgment.

But it's hard.

We want to hear that our parents are proud of us. We want our spouse to say thank you, to acknowledge what we do for them. We want to be made whole for what we've done, given, sacrificed. More than that, we want recognition, respect, we want appreciation, and when we do good things, we want credit.

Is that so unreasonable?

Here's an argument that it is: *You didn't do anything you weren't supposed to do.* As a talented and intelligent person, *it was your job* to do that thing. Whether it was a nice gesture or some difficult-to-pull-off feat, you did what you were capable of doing, what you were trained to do, what you were expected to do. You are supposed to be generous. You are supposed to be kind. The fact that no one is rushing to throw you a parade is its own compliment in a way. We're not surprised . . . because we know you. We know who you are.

Of course you did good! Of course you helped someone or cleaned something up or took the blame when it wasn't your fault.

Who better to do it than you?

What is surprising, or rather, *disappointing,* is to find out that you did it for the wrong reasons. That you were more self-involved than selfless. That it didn't come from a place of strength and generosity but of insecurity or thirst. There is nothing more desperate—and calculating—than a person who goes around thinking about "legacy." (As if anyone is around to enjoy posthumous fame.) They're ungrateful? No, it's ungrateful to expect more than the pleasure of knowing why you did what you did.

Do it with a smile. Be the beautiful person who just goes through the world doing their job, doing good, never expecting or asking for anything.

Think of the good Dorland could have done had she just moved on to the next good deed, instead of trying—in vain, it turns out—to earn an acquaintance's approval. Imagine if she had spent that energy convincing even more people to donate their kidneys, to keep the chain going. Wouldn't that have shut Larson up? Wouldn't it have been the ultimate refutation of anyone's cynicism and doubt?

But anyway, that was her call.

Let's just focus on doing the good we can do.

Let's forget about credit. Let's forget about gratitude.

We don't need anyone to appreciate us, to recognize us.

We do good because *we are good,* and everything else is extra.

Give Them Hope

⌒

Frederick Douglass had every reason to doubt. Every reason to be angry. He had seen not just the hypocrisy of human beings but their utter depravity, and had been the victim of it.

Even though he was now personally free, the struggle continued. Against Northern laborers who refused to work next to him in the shipyard, against schools that weren't open to his sons, against the indifference or incompetence of antislavery activists and politicians who seemed to want to do nothing but talk, talk, talk about the problem.

He kept going back—he kept fighting.

It had been years, years of this struggle, and how little progress to show for it, except for more days in what Martin Luther King Jr. would describe as the "cold and whistling winds of despair in a world sparked by turbulence." It was only natural that one day it would all pour out of him onstage, as it did in Salem, Ohio, in 1852 as he addressed an antislavery audience. His self-control failed him, his message grew dark and violent, all his hope seemed to fade away, and he railed at the injustice he knew so personally.

The audience was stunned. Douglass himself seemed like he was in a trance, being transformed from determined fighter to a hopeless nihilist before their eyes. But then a voice broke the gloomy silence of the room.

It was Sojourner Truth.

"Frederick," she called, "is God dead?"

These were magic words.

At his lowest point, Truth was giving her friend some hope. She was reminding him that he had no right to despair. That he should not deprive this audience of their zeal, of their vision of a better world.

It was the same lesson that Corrie ten Boom's sister tried to give with her last words as she lay dying in a concentration camp. "There is no pit so deep," her sister said of their God, "that He is not deeper still." Days later, Corrie would be released from Ravensbrück by a clerical error, narrowly escaping certain death. Had she given up . . . she would not have made it.

There was still goodness in the world then. There is still goodness now. God, whatever that means to you, is not dead.

Despair is a choice.

Cynicism is an excuse.

Neither create a better world.

Just as we fight against the status quo—cause good trouble

where necessary—so we must reject all forms of nihilism, un-seriousness, and despair.

"In this world goodness is destined to be defeated," Walker Percy would write his famous novel *The Moviegoer,* partly based on his beloved uncle's Stoic philosophy. While that doesn't sound hopeful, he meant it to be. "But a man must go down fighting," Percy wrote. "That is the victory."

To not let them break you. To keep going back. To focus on the progress that has been made, that is the victory.

Our north star is still up there, still shining. Let's follow it.

Historically, despair is actually the heresy anyway. Pick any point of time in the past, any that you like. Is not almost *everything* better now than it was then?

It's better because people made it better, people like you. It's better because there is always more at play than we can possibly know in the moment, because there is often something coming around the corner that we can't see when we are down and low.

Which is why we have to keep going, why we have to keep believing, why we cannot give in to despair.

Because where would we be if our heroes had? What if Gandhi had given up on nonviolence in 1940, faced with the prospect of the *world* going to war again for the second time in three decades? Not only would India's independence have been delayed or forever lost, but the rest of the century would have been an even more gruesome spectacle. What if Martin Luther

King Jr. had been deterred by those gruesome church bombings, if they had convinced him that the soul of America could not be redeemed? If Frederick Douglass had given up that day in Ohio, a decade before abolition?

Where will we be if *you* give up?

In November 1978, Harvey Milk sat down to record a message that would have tested the resolve of even the most dedicated activist. It was a message intended for the public but in the most extraordinary and depressing of contexts: He was crafting his final words, words to be played after the assassination that he had come to believe was almost inevitable. Yet even as he contemplated his own death at the hands of a bigot, he refused to concede or consider the death of the movement that was now so much bigger than him.

"I cannot prevent some people from feeling angry and frustrated and mad," he said of his murder, which would in fact happen just nine days after the date of the recording, "but I hope they will take that frustration and that madness and instead of demonstrating or anything of that type, I hope they would take the power and I would hope that five, ten, one hundred, a thousand would rise." They could not let their opponents win, he said, they could not let them break their spirit—because people *needed* them.

When you are forced to write your own last will and testament because you are convinced you're about to be killed, despair is a reasonable response. Yet Milk himself had said in his very first speech after being elected that while his constituents could not live on hope alone, life was not worth living without hope. So here, as he faced the potential of his own death, he held fast to that belief. He would not break that faith—indeed, as he spoke he did not waver, nor did his voice break or even pause.

Just the week before, he explained, he had gotten a call from someone in Altoona, Pennsylvania, who had been inspired by his election. "That's what this is all about," he said, wrapping up the last story he would ever get to tell. "It's not about personal gain, not about ego, not about power—it's about giving those young people out there in the Altoona, Pennsylvanias hope."

And then with his final words, he repeated that essential message, that obligation he wanted to hand to each and every person: "You gotta give them hope."

That's what de Gaulle did for France with his courage. That's what Gandhi did for India with his fundamental goodness. That's what we have to do in our own small way. It's our job, above all our other jobs.

Justice, like love, is not a victory march. It is a long, hard slog. It breaks hearts and bodies and relationships and pleasant fictions like they are twigs. Of course we have our doubts, of course we wonder if it's worth it, if we can do it.

No one is saying it's not dark out there. It may well get darker still.

But who will this despair help? It doesn't bring the dawn about, for sure. It doesn't encourage the good guys. It doesn't help your kids or your protégés. It does nothing for you or for people who deserve, who cry out for justice.

Don't let them kill the dream you dreamed.

We not only have to continue to hope, but we have to *bring* hope into the world.

We have to keep dreaming.

We have to carry the fire.

We have to not only keep others warm but help them light their own fires.

Be an Angel

H e had been persecuted. He had been ruined. He had been humiliated. Nearly everything that could be taken from a person had been taken from Oscar Wilde in 1895, including his freedom.

His wife, gone.

His children, he'd never see again.

His reputation, destroyed.

Even the copyrights to his writings had been taken.

For what? Because he loved another man? Because of unjust laws that would stand in England for another hundred years.

There he was, dragged from his prison cell to bankruptcy court, for one last hearing, one last abject degradation. A broken man, he walked, handcuffed, down the long prison corridor, jeered at and judged by the crowds who had gathered to see him brought low, the guards shoving him roughly to move faster.

His head sagged in shame for every step of the terrible journey, except once, just once Wilde looked up. And when he did he beheld a sight that he would store forever, he later wrote, in the treasure house of his heart, something "embalmed and kept sweet by the myrrh and cassia of many tears."

Robbie Ross, a fellow writer and old friend, had staked out a place in that horrible hallway so that he might offer something as small as a smile and a nod of respect to a man at his lowest moment. *I have not forsaken you,* he said wordlessly. *You are not alone,* he was saying with his presence. *You are not worthless. Do not give up.*

"When Wisdom has been profitless to me, and Philosophy barren, and the proverbs and phrases of those who have sought to give me consolation as dust and ashes in my mouth," Wilde reflected, "the memory of that little lowly act of Love has unsealed for me all the wells of pity, made the desert blossom like a rose, and brought me out of the bitterness of lonely exile into harmony with the wounded, broken, and great heart of the world."

Maybe that sounds like a bit much. But maybe that's because few of us have fallen that hard—going, as Wilde said of his life, from eating all the fruit from all the trees in the garden of the world to a dark dungeon of shame and pain.

What Robbie Ross did for Oscar Wilde was more than an act of friendship or loyalty, more than just the nothing that everyone else in his life had offered. It was an act of grace. Wilde himself would compare that act from his friend to the saints who washed the feet of the poor or kissed a leper.

Surveying the depravity that was the Holocaust, Israel sought to recognize the angels who saw evils and decided to try and stop them. "Righteous Among the Nations" is given out in recognition of non-Jews who saved Jews from extermination. Three queens have received it . . . but then again so have journalists, philosophers, and a department store employee. It's a reminder that decency knows no rank or social position, that the responsibility to do good is not limited to the powerful but stands there beckoning to all of us. Roughly thirty thousand people answered that call—angels, all of them.

And the vast majority of people who turned away? Who refused to acknowledge, let alone try and do anything to stop, the monstrous crime happening in front of them?

Call them what you like.

Ross's grace continued past the moment in the hallway.

When Wilde was released, Ross was there.

When the rights to Wilde's work went up for sale, Ross bought them all with his own money, managing a literary estate on behalf of Wilde's children. When Wilde lay dying, Ross was there again, summoning the priest and comforting him in his last hours.

The Carter family met a woman named Mary Prince when they moved into the Georgia governor's mansion in 1971. She had been assigned to their staff as part of a work program for incarcerated inmates. Rosalynn Carter quickly became convinced of Prince's innocence and was appalled at the details of her conviction—Prince, a black woman, had been convinced by her lawyer to plead guilty to manslaughter. The lawyer then had her plead to murder, for which she received a life sentence. The Carters asked that Prince be assigned to nanny their young daughter, Amy, and eventually secured her parole and a full pardon. She came to live with them in the White House. After his presidency, Carter bought her a house down the street from the Carters' in Plains, Georgia, and Prince, now in her late seventies, remains a close friend. Carter would dedicate a book called *Our Endangered Values* to her in 2006.

One official wrongly takes away someone's freedom . . . another welcomes a stranger into their family and fights for their freedom. Which will you be?

We should strive, Seneca once said, "to treat others as you wish the gods would treat you." Which is to say: With compassion. With endless patience. With infinite understanding. With love and generosity. God knows we need it . . . so at the very least we can try to give it.

Who knows if angels actually exist. What is true is that *you can do something close to that here on earth.*

You can be one of the good ones. Especially for the people you love and care about.

That's what Uncle Will was for Walker Percy—showing up, stepping in when he and his three brothers were orphaned. That's what Dean Acheson was trying to do when he refused to forsake Alger Hiss, even as part of him must have suspected his friend's guilt. He believed a higher obligation was at play, he explained, one stated long ago on "the Mount of Olives . . . in the 25th Chapter of the Gospel according to St. Matthew."

Acheson was referring, as it were, to those famous words that are supposed to constitute the bedrock of Christian charity and brotherhood: "Naked, and ye clothed me: I was sick, and ye visited me: I was in prison, and ye came unto me."

Forget who is to blame.

Forget what anyone else will think.

Think only, *There but for the grace of God go I . . .*

When everyone else has turned away, lean in.

Do what is kind and decent and so desperately needed.

That's what the parable of the Good Samaritan is about. It's not simply about helping, about offering charity or sympathy. It's about doing those things for someone whom everyone else has *refused* to help.

It's both superhuman and in fact very simple and very human. And so beautiful.

Our toughest assignment is here, in these moments where humanity is rare, where goodness is on the run. It's there that we step up, step in, stand with.

The nod in the hallway. Declining to pile on with the mob. The letter written to the prisoner. The guest bedroom offered to the person who just blew up their life.

If we don't do it, who will?

If we leave them hanging, leave them alone, leave them to wither and die, what does that say?

About the world? About us?

Forgive

When Jimmy Carter pardoned those who had fled conscription during the Vietnam War, he wasn't thinking of his political future. He was thinking of his simple Christian duty. He was trying to create reconciliation and peace.

And he was willing to sacrifice his own election prospects to achieve it.

That's a rare and beautiful thing.

The beauty—perhaps the secret power—of the civil rights movement was its belief in what came after. It was more than a power struggle, more than a fight for basic rights. It was instead a vision for the future, a belief in a better world that was not just possible but inevitable.

Keep your eyes on the prize, they said to each other. Keep your eyes on the prize.

Their price was also that same magical thing: *reconciliation.* The world of King's dream for his children, where blacks and whites could get along, could love each other, see the good in each other . . . despite the vicious evil and criminal deeds that whites had so recently been guilty of.

In short, it was a movement built around forgiveness.

The same standard of forgiveness that Jesus had so achingly set on the cross, crying out, as he did in his moment of agony: *Forgive them, Father, for they know not what they do.*

It was this standard that James Lawson brought down to earth not just as he trained a generation of young activists for the sit-ins, but also in 1968, after his beloved mentor and spiritual brother, Martin Luther King Jr., had been assassinated.

As a Christian and a true practitioner of the philosophy of nonviolence, Lawson felt called, in time, to meet and forgive King's assassin, James Earl Ray. In the years after the murder, Lawson spent a considerable amount of time with Ray, even coming to meet the man's fiancée. But for all this incredible forgiveness and restraint, Lawson understandably struggled when Ray took the astounding step of asking him to officiate his prison wedding.

It felt like too much. It was too painful. Was it unethical? Did it send the wrong message? So Lawson asked his family at dinner what they thought he should do. It was a short conversation. Almost before he could finish, Lawson's seventeen-year-old son was answering. "Well," his son said, not even needing to look up from his food, "if you believe all the stuff you've been preaching all these years, then you'll do it."

He was right. And Lawson did do it, presiding over the wedding of a man who had senselessly murdered his hero, showing not only grace but also proving who actually *won* in the battle against hatred and violence.

It's important to note that Jesus didn't just preach forgiveness on that one occasion on the cross. Before his death, he was asked about forgiveness by Peter. Knowing that forgiveness was important, Peter asked just how many times he should forgive his brother. Was it one time for one mistake? What if his brother did it again? What if he did it seven times? Should he forgive him seven times? "I do not say to you, up to seven times," Jesus replied, "but up to *seventy-seven times.*" In fact, according to some translations, Jesus actually said seventy *times* seven.

But even this understates it. The whole basis of Christianity is that because God has forgiven each person totally and completely, a Christian must in turn do the same. Whatever your spirituality, the same bargain stands: Someone kind, someone generous, someone we don't even know has forgiven us before at least once. In fact, life has given you *countless* second chances, chance after chance after chance. "Justice" would have cut you off along time ago—but here you are.

We carry that debt now, and so we must forgive others. Better yet, we have the power to enrich ourselves and the world by actively *investing* this forgiveness wherever possible, whenever we have the opportunity to provide grace to someone who has trespassed against us.

This is tough. It may well be the toughest thing there is.

Not necessarily in one moment of transformative grace—
we're not born saints. But we forgive little by little, day by day,
until we've let things go. We have to *work* on it. Remember, Marcus Aurelius caught himself getting better at wrestling, at ruling,
at everything but what he knew he needed to get better at—
being a better forgiver of faults. Forgiveness is more than just a
Christian tradition, it's part of the path of self-improvement too.
When Marcus was betrayed by his most trusted general, Avid-
ius Cassius, Marcus spoke of it as an opportunity to win the
"great prize both of war and of victory, a prize such as no human
being has ever yet obtained. And what is this prize? To forgive a
man who has wronged one, to remain a friend to one who has
transgressed friendship, to continue faithful to one who has
broken faith."*

Isn't that the beauty of Gandhi's life and the injustices he
endured? Because he chose love, forgiveness, and not clinging
to enmity, what came from them was not only justice for India,
but also a *playbook* for bringing about nonviolence—the one
that Lawson and King would themselves use. "Forgiveness," he
said, quoting an old proverb, "is the ornament of the brave."
Mercy, clemency—these are the finest robes a leader can dress
themselves in.

It's important, though, that we don't just dismiss this kind of

---

* His aim, he said, was to "settle this affair well and show to all mankind
that there is a right way to deal even with civil wars."

grace as somehow otherworldly, that only the true saints can pull it off. Plenty of people have pointed out that forgiveness is a gift we give foremost to ourselves. That's what the civil rights leaders figured out—that no one was more pitiable than these people they faced, so consumed with hate and anger that they could no longer even tell what a human being was.

"If I turned around every time somebody called me a faggot," Harvey Milk once said, "I'd be walking backwards, and I don't want to walk backwards." If he stewed about, held on to everything that had ever been said or done to him, never forgave or forgot the wrongs he experienced, how could he move forward? How could he possibly have anything to be hopeful about, let alone give hope to others?

And so must you. You'll never get that pound of flesh . . . except out of your own skin. You can't possibly hang on to this forever.

You're going to have to let go, to be bigger, to be better. You're going to have to understand, forgive, *love.*

For them. For you. For the world.

It is the only way. It is *the* way.

Forgiveness is not martyrdom—it is a kind of conquering, transcending the opponent, the situation, and yourself.

Nothing frustrates evil quite like forgiveness. Nothing befuddles hatred quite like not getting hatred in return.

So we'll wield this grace as a weapon, for ourselves and the world.

Make Amends

~

John Profumo was a reckless, entitled, and irresponsible man. Even just the sound of his name evokes this history, so permanently associated is it in British politics with scandal and shame. Rightfully so: The Profumo affair, as it's known, involved John cheating on his wife with a nineteen-year-old showgirl, lying to Parliament about it, and through this disgrace and very real national security concerns bringing about the fall of the British prime minister.

Profumo resigned in shame, driven from public and political life.

But instead of railing against what today we might call "cancel culture," planning a comeback, or cashing in with a tell-all memoir, Profumo did something very different.

Just weeks after his resignation, Profumo appeared at Toynbee Hall, a poverty-fighting charity in England. Asking if he might be of help, he was promptly handed some dirty laundry, a humble assignment that changed his life forever.

He would go on to be Toynbee Hall's single longest-serving volunteer, working his way up from manual labor to its chief fund-raiser, putting in thousands upon thousands of hours over the next forty years, almost entirely without recognition or fanfare.

May we all respond to life's twists with such quiet class and goodness.

This idea of making amends, of atoning for sins or failings, is one that most of us are surprisingly bad at—surprising, because you'd think as such inherently imperfect people we might have at least perfected the art of addressing our mistakes. Certainly, our long list of blunders and transgressions should have provided ample opportunity to get good at it.

Even Gandhi knew he wasn't perfect. He was quick to admit error. He was quick to hold himself accountable—if anything he took it too far, atoning almost all his life for the sin he supposedly committed while his father died.

There is no justice without the ability to acknowledge mistakes and take responsibility for your actions.

There is a story about Lincoln, who well before the Civil War had had been mocked at an event by a political opponent named Jesse Thomas. Lincoln, hearing of the insults, rushed across town to address the crowd before they left. There, in rare form, he began with an almost perfect impression of Thomas, mimicking how the man walked and talked. The crowd, loving every minute of it, roared with laughter. Lincoln, riding their energy, kept going, ridiculing and criticizing Thomas so thoroughly that one witness described it as a public "skinning," made all the more painful by the fact that Thomas was trapped sitting in the audience, observing his own humiliation. Thomas would leave in tears.

As the event became the talk of Springfield, Lincoln quickly realized how cruel he had been, even though he had not struck first nor intended to hurt anyone. It had been so easy for a man of his intelligence and talents to be clever (and entertaining), but it had been harder for him to see how terribly unkind it was. On his own, he tracked down Thomas and repented. But more than a simple apology, he carried with him the lesson of what it meant to take things too far, even years later still thinking back to the moment "with the deepest chagrin."

More important, the Lincoln that came out of this exchange was a wiser, more patient, more forgiving man—closer to the man who would build his second inaugural address not only around the undeniable sins of the slaveholding South but also the complicity and responsibility of the North.

For some reason, nearly two hundred years later, we're still struggling with this, still struggling to even *acknowledge* the sins of the past that *other people* committed. The state of Virginia apologized for slavery . . . in 2007! The first state in America to do so! How many Northern states—whose banks and factories were just as much a part of the same system—would conceive of needing to make a similar apology? For this reason, "reparations" has become one of the dirtiest words in American politics, when it could actually be seen as a beautiful idea, one that, even if impractical, is redemptive even to discuss.

Not that America is unique. Turkey refuses to even say the word "genocide" in regard to the deportation and killing of hundreds of thousands of Armenians. Japan has never fully acknowledged its terrible use of "comfort women" and the other sexual crimes of its empire. The Catholic Church spent decades covering up and denying its own terrible abuse scandals. The whole world owes an apology to gay people.

In some cases, there is no one even alive who is directly guilty for these grave injustices, yet still, no one wants to look them directly in the face. Not being guilty does not absolve one of responsibility. But refusing to see it, covering it up, that does make you complicit. It makes you morally responsible when it happens again.

The Germans have a word—*Vergangenheitsbewältigung*—which means to grapple with the past, with collective responsibility for injustice. Across Germany there are some seventy-five thousand *Stolpersteine,* or stumbling stones, small raised markers that note injustices—in most cases, *murders*—related to the Holocaust. Again, the vast majority of people bumping into these stones, which have been inserted into sidewalks and roads, would not have even been alive when the horrible crimes behind them were committed. But like with slavery, the implications of these crimes continue, the injustices still exist.

While we cannot change the past, we can—by refusing to deny it—do better in the future. In so doing, we begin to make amends for what has happened.

And we *must* make these amends. We must heal and improve and set things on a better path.

Speaking about colonialism, the missionary, philosopher, and Nobel Peace Prize winner Dr. Albert Schweitzer would explain that his tireless work in medical clinics in Africa was premised on the idea that "we are burdened with a great debt. We are not free to confer or not confer these benefits on these people as we please. It is our *duty*. Anything we give them is not benevolence but atonement. That is the foundation from which all deliberations about 'works of mercy' must begin."

Whether it was a cruel exchange like Lincoln or an affair like Profumo or a propensity for childhood bullying or the way we acted at some point in our marriage, each of us has to have the courage to grapple with the past. Our collective and our personal pasts. We have to have the strength not just to acknowledge error but to make things better.

While nothing can undo what has been done, we always have the opportunity to do *better*. We have the opportunity to become a better person as a result of what has happened, even if that is only through having to step up and own the unpleasant responsibility for it.

Denial, defiance, disavowal—this is insecurity. It's weak people, weak societies who will not try to make things right. Who think they can't afford to apologize or make reparations.

Just as we must try to forgive those who trespass against us, we must make an active effort to seek forgiveness for the trespasses we have made. We can't pretend it didn't happen.

We have to make amends.

We owe it to those who have been hurt.

We also owe it to ourselves.

Our potential is not reached by running from things, it's by grappling with them—especially the difficult ones.

What we did, what has happened, it doesn't have to be a secret shame, it doesn't have to be a seeping wound, a weight that's dragging us down.

It can be something that transforms us, a vehicle for redemption and improvement.

It can make us . . . and the world . . . a more just place.

The Great Oneness

~

In 1950, a man grieving his young son who had just died of polio got a letter from Albert Einstein. Now, one might think that as a man of science, Einstein would have had a rather resigned view of the tragic nature of the human condition.

We're born. We're buffeted by forces beyond our control, beyond our comprehension, and then we die.

Often for no reason, leaving profound suffering in its wake.

Given the immensity of the events of the middle of the twentieth century—the Holocaust and the violence of the atomic age—it was quite reasonable that Einstein might be inured to the loss of a single child to whom he had no relation.

Instead, Einstein's letter was one of profound and philosophic condolence.

"A human being," he wrote, "is a part of the whole, called by us 'Universe,' a part limited in time and space. He experiences himself, his thoughts and feelings as something separated from the rest—a kind of optical delusion of his consciousness. The striving to free oneself from this delusion is the one issue of true religion. Not to nourish the delusion but to try to overcome it is the way to reach the attainable measure of peace of mind."

Einstein was expressing one of the few things that physics and philosophers and priests seem to agree on: That everything and everyone is far more connected than we are prone to think. We shared an animating force, an energy, a unity that no matter what happens or how different things seem is always there. Even in our suffering, in our grief, we are tapping into something eternal and vast, something that makes us realize we are very much not alone.

"You think your pain and your heartbreak are unprecedented in the history of the world," James Baldwin wrote, "and then you read." It was books, history, philosophy, Baldwin said, that taught him that "the things that tormented me were the very things that connected me with all the people who were alive, or who had ever been alive."

We are all one.

It's so easy to forget it, but it's true.

No one has felt this more profoundly than the astronauts who had the unique experience of seeing the Earth from space. Whether they were American or Russian or Chinese, they were all overwhelmed by what has been called the "overview effect," an instantaneous global consciousness, an inescapable sense that everyone is in the same boat, no matter where they live or what they believe.

What they experienced looking at the "Blue Marble" that is

our planet was the exact thing that Hierocles was trying to teach people about two thousand years ago. Yes, we naturally think of ourselves and the people we love first, but with work, we can expand that circle of concern larger and larger until we see everything that is alive as one enormous organism. Astronauts experience the exact same thing that Gandhi, who never even flew in a plane, never saw humanity from above more than few stories up in a building, called *the great oneness.*

Realizing this, letting it wash over us, sitting in awe of it—it's more than just humbling. It also makes us more generous, more courageous, more committed to what's right. It makes us less concerned with petty nonsense, with meaningless distinctions, with grudges or our own pain.

It's euphoric. It can also be existentially devastating.

The actor William Shatner, after a lifetime of exploring space on film, finally visited the cosmos at age ninety. He thought he'd marvel at the beauty of all that he beheld. Instead, looking at the Earth from afar, all he felt was sadness.

Because, he realized, everything that mattered was down there on Earth and everyone was taking it for granted. They were destroying this thing of beauty, abusing it, stealing it from generations unborn.

The garment of interdependence, the great bundle of humanity that Frances Ellen Watkins Harper spoke of, it's real. But what kind of shape is it in these days? The environment is reeling. Billions live in poverty. Millions perish of totally preventable causes. Injustice tears at the fabric that binds us together. How long can it go unchecked before everything comes apart?

> I am convinced that people are much better off when their whole city is flourishing than when certain citizens prosper but the community has gone off course. When a man is doing well for himself but his country is falling to pieces, he goes to pieces along with it, but a struggling individual has much better hopes if his country is thriving.

Is that the lament of a modern politician? The manifesto of some early-twentieth-century socialist revolutionary?

No, it's Pericles in 431 BC.

The whole point of government and the social contract is built around this idea. All government, it was said by one of the Founders, has as its sole goal the common welfare.

What good is our success if it comes at the expense of others? How safe are we if our safety leaves others vulnerable? What good are we if we can't help others? We are all bound up in this thing called life together. We share this planet together. When we forget that, or lose track of how our own actions affect others, that's when injustice flourishes.

Marcus Aurelius's line that "what's bad for the hive is bad for the bee" could just as easily be a quip in an upcoming political debate as it could be a *New York Times* op ed. It's something that he needed constant reminders of, just as we do. He strove to see the world "as a living being—one nature and soul ... [where] everything feeds into that single experience, moves with a single motion. And how everything helps produce everything else. Spun and woven together." Did his policies and decisions always reflect that? No. And his biggest failings—the persecution of the Christians by the Romans at that time—are a reflection of what happens when we lose track of that ultimate north star.

"I am not conscious of a single experience throughout my three month stay in England and Europe," Gandhi observed after one of his visits, "that made me feel that after all East is East and West is West. On the contrary, I have been convinced more than ever that human nature is much the same, no matter what clime it flourishes."

This was why he couldn't hate. Why he couldn't turn his back. Why he dreamed of a better world with fewer divisions, where problems were never solved by violence or domination. "Life will not be a pyramid with an apex sustained by the bottom," he explained, sounding like Hierocles. "But it will be an oceanic circle whose centre will be the individual always ready to perish for the village, the latter ready to perish for the circle of villages, till at last the whole becomes one life composed of individuals, never aggressive in their arrogance but ever humble, sharing the majesty of the oceanic circle of which they are integral units."

This is what the last years of his life were dedicated to, why he was willing to die not just for independence but for equality for the untouchables and for Muslim and Hindu peace. "I am a Muslim," he said, "a Hindu, a Buddhist, a Christian, a Jew, a Parsi."

And so are you. We all are.

We are one and the same.

All mortal. All flawed.

All gifted with incredible potential. All deserving of justice and respect and dignity.

All unique individuals and yet an inseparable part of humanity, of the past, present, and future.

Truman kept a line from a Milton poem in his wallet that read simply:

The parliament of Man, the federation of the world.

That's what we belong to. That's what we must protect.

Expand the Circle

~

At the 1932 Summer Olympics in Los Angeles, a flashy Japanese equestrian named Shunzo Kido gave one of the most remarkable performances in the history of sport. He managed to grab the lead in a twenty-two-and-a-half-mile, fifty-obstacle endurance race that he didn't normally compete in. That his horse wasn't even trained for.

A teammate had been injured and Kido replaced him. But then suddenly, clear of the pack and over the second-to-last jump, a gold medal nearly within his grasp, he pulled the reins and dropped out of the race.

Why?

Some part of him sensed that the horse could not take any more, that although he could win, the horse would not survive the victory. As the plaque on the Friendship Bridge along California's Mount Rubidoux Trail commemorating his unprecedented display of sportsmanship reads, "Lt. Col. Shunzo Kido turned aside from the prize to save his horse. He heard the low voice of mercy, not the loud acclaim of glory."

How we treat the people who work for us, how we treat strangers, this says a lot about us.

How we treat the defenseless? The voiceless? Other species? According to Gandhi, it says *everything* about us. *Whatever you have done to the least of my brethren.*

In Milan Kundera's *The Unbearable Lightness of Being,* written about the Prague Spring and the Soviet military occupation, Tereza, the sensitive and compassionate female protagonist, tells her husband, "It is much more important to dig a half-buried crow out of the ground than to send petitions to a president."

Of course, politics matter. Of course, the big fights of our time matter. But so do the very little things that we hardly see. The Jains of India, a religion that dates back the sixth century BC and emphasizes respect for all living beings, would, as a rule, not make their pilgrimages during the rainy season, because they didn't want to trample on the new grass underfoot. What a beautiful and kind practice to build one's plans around, a practical as well as a metaphorical reminder that even our smallest choices ripple through the world around us. It was certainly influential to Gandhi, whose vegetarianism was the mother of all his other compassionate decisions.

One ancient philosopher would say that kindness was bigger than justice, because justice was about the law, about human beings, but kindness was also about how we treat animals and all living creatures. That's what the Stoics were trying to do—to expand the definition of who they owed kindness and justice to.

Leonardo da Vinci is known for his brilliant paintings and creations. But his friends? They knew him as the kind of person who would see a caged bird in a market and buy it, only so he could let it free. Before Lincoln even knew what slavery was, his moral empathy was awakened when his younger stepbrother John Daniel Johnston caught a turtle and smashed it against a tree for fun. The turtle's painful and pointless death was too much for the boy, who began, his stepsister reflected, to "preach against cruelty to animals, contending that an ant's life was to it, as sweet as ours to us." So of course, years later, when Lincoln first saw slaves chained together—"strung together precisely like so many fish upon a trot-line," as he vividly described it—he was just as appalled. This was no way to treat anyone or anything.

Of course, it's easier not to stop and think about what it must be like for a bird to be in a cage. It's easier to think only of the smell when you pass a factory farm, to think only of price as you're weighing two very differently sourced items at the supermarket. It's a pain to stop to catch a dog in the street. But just as we must concern ourselves about how the other half lives, we must consider the lives of the billions and billions of other life forms on this planet.

Have you watched the famous video where Koko the Gorilla, after years of watching Mr. Rogers on television, finally gets to meet the man? In an instant, she reaches down to remove his famous blue shoes—a gesture of neighborliness from across the animal kingdom, a reminder that evolution has given many species the capacity for kindness too.

And as a result obligated us to be kind too.

Cato the Elder, Cato's great-grandfather, was judged in his own time for the way he used up the animals that worked his farm. Not content with simply benefiting from their labor, he worked them to death and then replaced them. It was plenty legal and surely profitable, but that didn't make it right.

It's good that we recoil when we hear it, as we do when we look at an old map and learn that just a few generations ago, our ancestors divvied up an entire continent by what they could take from it—the Gold Coast, the Ivory Ghost, the Slave Coast.

It's naive to think that these impulses, this crude exploitation has simply disappeared. We must examine the thoughtless, profitable cruelties in our own way of living, in our businesses and do our best to resolve them . . . or at least mitigate them. The work of Temple Grandin, for instance, has helped reduce the suffering in slaughterhouses, just as the work of animal rights activists has challenged millions of people to question whether they should be eating meat at all. Both have different understandings of what justice is in this case, but both are making the world a better place.

The same goes for hunters and farmers, who have radically different relationships with wildlife, but than environmentalists in the best cases have found common cause in the preservation of endangered species, the climate, and the world that we all enjoy. Just as each person ought to be able to sit under their own fig tree and not be afraid, so should the majestic wildlife on this planet—animals that have been here far longer than us—be allowed to survive and thrive and do what they do.

And not just the majestic species or the cute ones . . . the fig tree itself deserves protection. The vine deserves rich soil. The rivers should flow unpolluted. The grass should be able to grow so high that it bends under its own weight, as Marcus Aurelius once observed. The whole world is a temple, the Stoics said. Nature is god—we commit a sacrilege when we abuse it.

"A man is really ethical," Albert Schweitzer wrote, "only when he obeys the constraint laid on him to help all life which he is able to succor, and when he goes out of his way to avoid injuring anything living. He does not ask how far this or that life deserves sympathy as valuable in itself, nor how far it is capable of feeling. To him life as such is sacred." That's what made Schweitzer a vegetarian . . . and to put aside most of his philosophic work to run medical clinics in Africa.

Ehrfurcht vor dem Leben was the beautiful phrase that came to him on a boat trip on the Ogooué River in what is now Gabon, Africa. *A reverence for life.*

We have to care about all life forms . . . even though our lives are besieged by so many more personal or urgent cares. Because it says something about us. Because it is a legacy we will leave the future . . . in fact, it may well determine whether there *is* a future.

It should not surprise us that Cato, so uninterested in the lives of the animals he owned, was also a ruthless slave owner. Which is sort of the point. The logic that says some humans are less important than others—because they don't look like us, because they live far away from us, because they're not related to us—is the same logic that says other forms of life are less important.

This is not only anathema to the principles of justice. It's corrupting and dangerous to the person who holds it. Unkindness, indifference, cruelty in one area . . . bleeds over. It's also the opportunity: The more we open our hearts in one area, the more open we can be in others.

By "expanding the circle," as the philosopher Peter Singer terms it, we make the world better.

We also make ourselves better.

Find the Good in Everyone

~

I f Harvey Milk had been a little more closed-minded, he might still be alive.

But if he had been a little more closed-minded, he wouldn't have been Harvey Milk.

Most people, even before his fatal clash with Milk, thought there was something off about Dan White, a former police officer turned local politician with very strong antigay views.

"Harvey, the guy's a pig," a neighbor had told him.

But Harvey insisted that it was simply a matter of ignorance. "He's working class, a Catholic, been brought up with all those prejudices," Milk explained, defending a man he had little reason to defend. "I'm gonna sit next to him every day and let him know we're not all those bad things he thinks we are."

People told him he was wasting his time. People told him he would regret it. *Some men you just can't reach* ...

Milk tried anyway. It was part of his philosophy of creating allies.

"As the years pass," Harvey argued, "the guy can be educated ...

everyone can be educated and helped. *You* think some people are hopeless—not me."

Indeed, they would find common ground, becoming friends, working together to do things, despite their very different experiences. It was White who got Milk appointed to chairman of the Streets and Transportation Committee board. Milk would attend the baptism of White's child in 1977. White would support the first and only law Milk passed, and he would also come out against a measure that was intended to allow local school boards to fire openly gay teachers.

And then White, after a series of disagreements with Milk and the city's mayor, would shoot Milk five times, the final two bullets point-blank into Milk's skull.

Did kindness work? Was it worth it?

That's not a question Milk would have asked.

The question was whether it was right. Was about which path had the most heart, held the most hope.

If Harvey Milk had seen only the bigotry in people, had seen only the dangers they represented, well, then he never could have allied with the Teamsters to begin with. He certainly wouldn't have been able to find hope in anyone or anything, certainly wouldn't have been able to give it to people.

Each of us has a Hitler inside us, Dr. Edith Eger would later write, as well as a Corrie ten Boom (one of the Righteous Among the Nations honorees). Which one will we let out? Which one will we choose to see in others?

In one of his many prison terms in South Africa, Gandhi passed the time by making sandals. One of these pairs, as he left Africa for India in 1914, he gave to General Jan Smuts, the prime minister of South Africa, with whom he had tangled so many times and who had personally sent him to jail.

Smuts would go on to fight in both world wars. He would become a leading politician of his time. Yet all the while, he was thinking of Gandhi, especially when, exactly as Gandhi had intended, he put on those sandals. Thinking of Gandhi's grace, his moral call, his courage. On Gandhi's seventieth birthday, Smuts would give the sandals back. "I have worn these sandals for many a summer since then," he reflected, "even though I may feel that I am not worthy to stand in the shoes of so great a man." In fact, Smuts, despite his earlier complicity in a racist and exploitative system, did a worthy job filling those shoes. He was instrumental in the founding of the League of Nations. He wrote the draft of the UN Charter two decades later. He helped find a homeland for the Jews after the Holocaust.

It was Gandhi, he said, who had redeemed him, delivered him from "a sense of commonplace and futility," serving for him and all mankind as an "inspiration . . . not to weary in well doing."

"You must not lose faith in humanity," Gandhi would later write to Amrit Kaur, India's first health minister after independence. He was reassuring her but also reminding himself. "Humanity is an ocean. If a few drops of the ocean are dirty, the ocean does not become dirty."

The whole premise of Gandhi's philosophy was that there was goodness in other people—or at least in *most* people. No one was an untouchable to him, no one was too far gone, not worth lobbying for. That's what nonviolence depended on, what it appealed to. It worked on the British because for all the riches the empire had reaped from colonialism, they were ashamed of their greed and cruelty when it was reflected back at them. And after enough shame—shame Gandhi himself was no stranger to in his own life—they agreed to change. Better still, they tried to do better.

He had plenty of reason to lose faith in humanity. The civil rights protestors and the suffragettes all did too. Day-to-day they saw the *worst* of people . . . yet they look past that, they kept their eyes on the prize, continued to appeal to and believe in their opponents' humanity, which many others quite reasonably concluded did not exist. And it was in doing this, by creative witness, by courageous resistance, by demonstrating their own humanity that these activists slowly coaxed out that humanity from their otherwise cruel oppressors. You don't just look for the good, you *find* it. Because it's there—however well covered. In each wrongdoer, in each stranger, in all people, Marcus Aurelius would explain, there is a nature similar to our own. There is good in each of them, a role they were meant to play in our life.

This will challenge us, make us vulnerable, scare us, as Marcus knew firsthand. With love, Marcus would write about how even his flawed stepbrother helped him improve his own character. Still, his brother must have also frustrated him, must have repeatedly let him down.

With grace, Marcus would use his experience with Cassius, his longtime friend who betrayed him, as a chance to teach and grow as a leader. We'll all be dead before long, Marcus reminded himself . . . and besides, they haven't really hurt us, they haven't changed *our* ability to be just and good.

Mickey Schwerner was a young Jewish kid who went South during the Freedom Summer. He taught school. He registered voters. He tried to get people jobs. For this, he found himself brutalized by the police and then kidnapped and taken to a dark rural road at gunpoint. In his final moments on earth, facing torture and death, one captor grabbed him and asked, "Are you that n*gger lover?"

And Mickey looked him in the eye and said with with his last words, "Sir, I know just how you feel."

His murderers told themselves many things—that Mickey was an agitator, that Mickey was a race traitor, that Mickey was a communist, that Mickey was a godless outsider set to destroy their way of life.

The author William Bradford Huie had a remarkable confrontation with one of the men who murdered Mickey then buried his limp body in a levee with two other activists, sure to never be discovered.

"It's true that he called himself an atheist," Huie explained.

"He did, huh? He didn't believe in *nothing*?"

"Oh yes," Huie replied. "He believed in something. He believed devoutly."

"What'd he believe in?"

"He believed in *you*!"

"In me! What the hell!"

"Yeah. He believed in you. He believed that love could conquer hate. He believed love could change even you. He didn't think you were hopeless. That's what got him killed."

It's true, much of the time we will find ourselves disappointed. It's what got Harvey Milk killed too. We will sometimes find that the good we searched for in a person pales in comparison to the darkness or cruelty that exists alongside it.

We will suffer for this benefit of the doubt, for this forgiveness, this hope. Yet it must spring from us eternal. Even though it will not be returned.

We cannot see people as fixed. We cannot see them as all bad.

Because if we do then it means our job is done. It means change is impossible. It means justice is dead.

The lyrics to "Amazing Grace," you know them, yes?

Amazing grace, how sweet the sound
That saved a wretch like me.
I once was lost, but now I'm found,
Was blind, but now I see.

The man who wrote them, John Newton, was a broken and flawed man. He was cruelly conscripted into the British navy against his will, where he was beaten and whipped and abused. He paid back this abuse by becoming a cruel conscripter himself, serving as a captain of a slave ship on countless voyages.

Plenty of reason to write a person off, to label them irredeemably broken or evil.

But Newton eventually became a fervent abolitionist, a critical part of Thomas Clarkson's campaign, an ally without whom change may not have been possible.

People are worse than we'd like. They are also better than we can possibly comprehend. That's the power of grace.

It's why we sit with the Dan Whites, even at our peril. Even though it often doesn't work.

Because we can't afford to lose the times it does work.

Because *we* are improved by the hope and the patience and the faith of it.

Give the Full Measure of Devotion

When Regulus returned to Carthage as a voluntary prisoner, his captors didn't throw him a parade for keeping his word. The man who had left his weeping family, who had gotten to spend just a few days in his beloved homeland after so many years, was not treated mercifully by his captors out of respect for his awesome principles.

No, they tortured him. *To death.*

As he knew they would.

The kindest story of his execution was a crucifixion. One of the worst has Regulus deprived of sleep until he lost his mind, his misery ending only when he was trampled to death by an elephant.

He had gone willingly to Carthage, sure that this "manifest destruction" awaited him. He upheld his word, for the same reason Gandhi had voluntarily returned to jail after being given a week to bury his beloved wife. Sure, they could have escaped—it would have been better for them if they had—but that's why they didn't.

As a representative of Rome, Regulus's oaths, his decisions were not just about him. "My reasons for this attitude are various," Regulus explained, "but the principal one is that if I abide by my oath, I alone shall suffer disaster, but if I break it, the whole city will be involved." He would gladly suffer now himself than defer that cost to generations of future Romans whose word no friend or foe could trust.

Emily Davison, who endured imprisonment and a grueling, near-fatal hunger strike before her final act of political sacrifice, throwing herself in front of the king's horse, explained "I did it deliberately and with all my power, because I felt that by nothing but the sacrifice of human life would the nation be brought to realise the horrible torture our women face!"

Gerald Ford didn't *want* to destroy his chance at reelection, but he felt that the principles of clemency, of reconciliation, and of good governance demanded that he pardon his predecessor, Richard Nixon. Not that Nixon was particularly gracious about it, not that the country particularly understood the sacrifice at play. But he did it. Just as Carter after him would use the same power for an equally costly moment of grace.

At Yorktown in 1781, Thomas Nelson could see the British invaders coming close. When his orders came to fire, he did not flinch, telling the gunners to aim for the stately home that the British had occupied near the waterfront on Main Street. As he dialed in their aim, offering a reward of five guineas for anyone who hit it, few of the artillerymen could have guessed that their commander was helping them destroy *his own home.*

Some are asked to give a little. Some a lot. Some are asked to give *everything.*

When we have our north star, it makes it clear what we must do. Our strong sense of self allows us to be selfless. Even when it is painful, even when it is costly.

Clarity, of course, does not make such a sacrifice *easy.*

Regulus must have doubted himself, as any human being would have. Not just when he was in the sheer agony of his torture, or the long, lonely journey back to his painful fate. But also in those tortured moments of consideration, as he wrestled with his competing obligations—the kind we all have, because work, family, country, honor are not always going to be aligned. It was awful enough that the man had to swear off seeing his wife in the first days after returning to Rome, knowing that his love might override his duty. Can you imagine what he felt as his children clung to his leg, as his friends begged him to reconsider, as they told him he didn't *have* to do it, that no one would judge him for staying?

But he went anyway . . . and according to Seneca, even after that horrible death, Regulus would have done it again if given the chance, as one suspects Carter and Ford and King and Gandhi would have. "Do you wish to know how little he regrets that he set virtue at such a price?" Seneca wrote of Regulus, calling him not wretched but *happy.* "Set him free from the cross and send him back to the senate: he will state the same opinion."

"I wouldn't take my own life," Martin Luther King Jr. once explained of his own commitment, "but I would willingly give my life for that which I think is right."

Regulus wasn't around to experience the benefits of his commitment, but generations of his countrymen did. His enemies too. People knew *you could trust a Roman's word to the death.*

It almost never works to the benefit of whistleblowers who come forward. They pay a fortune in legal fees, lose their jobs, lose years of their life.

Abolishing slavery is said to have cost Britain roughly 2 percent of its GDP for the next *half century.* That would be a number measured ultimately in the trillions of dollars and the British government was still making payments as late as 2015. But in retrospect, was there any other way?

Because there is a cost the other way too, it should be noted. One pays for their selfishness, Oscar Wilde reminds us in *The Picture of Dorian Grey,* "in remorse, in suffering, in . . . well, in the consciousness of degradation."

Hopefully the good we do, the cost we pay will be appreciated. Maybe it will not.

Maybe people will understand. Maybe not. But it isn't about that. It's not about us at all. It's about the people who depend on us.

Besides, we're not after the third thing here . . . which is good because we may not be around when people eventually come around to giving it.

All that matters is that we do what matters.

Harvey Milk's selflessness wasn't just about the people he was trying to give hope to, although it was for them that he was willing to face his own sense of impending death.

But Milk's final choice was also an act of selfless giving, one that is practical and attainable to all of us. Because when Milk died, per his request, his organs were donated—as all of us have the opportunity to agree in life to give in death.

Even if he had never saved from suicide closeted gays he'd encouraged to come out, even if he had never promoted peace and harmony between radically different lifestyles and faiths, from this final choice alone, he still would have been a hero, a giver of hope and happiness . . . as you can be too.

By checking a simple box on a form.

By committing yourself in what you do, big and small, to being a giver. To value other people more than yourself.

To value what is right more than your life.

To give the full measure of our devotion, that's what we're here for.

That's the job. That's justice.

Love Wins

~

Malcolm X was an angry man.
Newspapers would describe him as the angriest man in America. It was a charge he did not deny.

It was perfectly understandable. Before even getting to the terrible injustices of the country at that time, this is a man who was born into poverty. His father died, tragically, gruesomely, when Malcolm was just six years old. Malcolm was sucked into the criminal underworld and spent years in a dank prison.

And there was the fact that racism, it was always there. At age thirteen, his eighth-grade teacher asked him what he wanted to do with his life. Malcolm, smart and a clever speaker, said he wanted to be a lawyer. This teacher, one whom Malcolm admired and looked up to, crushed the earnestness out of him in a heartbreaking moment. "You've got to be realistic about being a n*gger," the man told him. "A lawyer—that's no realistic goal for a n*gger."

Imagine a life with so much misfortune and cruelty. Imagine

a thousand humiliations and disappointments. Imagine a world where you are legally a second-class citizen. Imagine a world where all this is enforced with the ever-present threat of violence and death.

So yeah, he was angry. So yeah, a product of hate, he hated.

"The most terrible thing about it," Wilde would write from a dark prison cell not unlike the one that Malcolm knew, "is not that it breaks one's heart." Hearts were made to be broken, after all. The truly terrible thing about injustice, he said, is "that it turns one's heart to stone."

In prison, Malcolm started to read. He read philosophy and history. He was like Gandhi in England—he soaked up everything. But as Gandhi knew, there was a potential danger in all this learning. It can destroy what's left of one's illusions. Gandhi was once asked what worried him the most in life, and his answer was simply, "the hardness of heart of the educated." The truth that Malcolm learned in those books, what he learned about what people had been doing to his people for hundreds and hundreds of years, it had precisely that effect.

Malcolm converted to a separatist sect of Islam, the Nation of Islam, that preached radical black supremacy. The phrase "The white man is the devil," which he heard as part of his religious conversion, rang true against nearly every experience he had had in his life, everything he'd read about. It was almost inevitable, Malcolm would later reflect, that he'd respond to that idea and that "the next twelve years of [his] life were devoted and dedicated to propagating that phrase among black people."

Malcolm quickly rose through their ranks of the Nation of Islam, emerging from jail as one of the most provocative and passionate speakers of his generation. But unlike Martin Luther King Jr., his message was violent. It was bitter. It was driven by anger and not hope.

At one particularly low point in 1961, he found himself, at the order of Elijah Muhammad, the leader of the Nation of Islam, discussing a collaboration with the Ku Klux Klan. Two radically different worldviews, yes, but at opposite ends of the horseshoe, alarmingly close to each other.

Malcolm had every reason to be angry.

The problem is that it didn't really get him anywhere.

Not only was he slowly eaten up by the hate he felt, but the Nation of Islam was paralyzed by it too. Sure, they wrote and spoke eloquently about the injustices of America at that time. But they desegregated no lunch counters. Despite all their talk about fighting back, in actuality they waged no battles and fought no wars. In fact, all their righteous anger was betrayed by Elijah Muhammad, who was enriching himself and chasing women.

In *Meditations*, Marcus Aurelius would write that "what doesn't transmit light creates its own darkness." When we close ourselves off to love and hope, naturally we experience less love and hope. "Whoever hardens their heart," the Bible reminds us, "falls into trouble." We create our own darkness.

Both these ideas capture perfectly the trap that Malcolm X found himself in.

Many of us, subject to far less severe circumstances, do the same thing. But we have to resist, to make room for love.

Think of where Gandhi was at the end. Not only had he seen nearly eighty years of injustice and struggle, but when he finally succeeded, he found not the Elysian Fields but violence on a scale he could not have even imagined. His longtime allies abandoned the sole force that had brought them to their victory. His own people turned on each other, bringing violence to his literal doorstep.

He would have had every reason to despair, to give up.

He could have, maybe even should have, been angrier than Malcolm. Which makes the final days of his life even more beautiful and perfect. He held true. "No cause that is intrinsically just can ever be described as forlorn," he wrote. He loved. He kept his heart open. He *gave* more. It was his greatest performance, his final sermon.

Given that Malcolm X died by the very violence he preached, one might be mistaken that his story ended in darkness, that he left this world with a hardened heart.

Quite the opposite.

At age thirty-nine, driven from the Nation of Islam but still a believer in his faith, Malcolm visited Mecca. There, broken and angry, he found himself open, receptive to light that he had previously believed had gone out of the world.

He met world leaders and ordinary people alike. He met with Christians and Muslims. He met with white people who treated him with respect, people who shared the same faith as he did. He realized for the first time that not everyone was a racist, that perhaps the world was not actually a war of all against all but a place where most people are trying the best they can, that there was more love out there than he thought.

"I've had enough of someone else's propaganda," he wrote home. "I'm for truth, no matter who tells it. I'm for justice, no matter who is for or against. I'm a human being first and foremost, and as such I'm for whoever and whatever benefits humanity *as a whole*."

After his time in Mecca, his life expanded—he brought into his circle of friends Christians and Jews and Buddhists and Hindus and unbelievers alike. "True Islam," he would reflect after, "taught me that it takes *all* of the religious, political, economic, psychological and racial ingredients, or characteristics, to make the Human Family and the Human Society complete."

It was this larger perspective, this experience that he brought back to the streets of Harlem in 1964 that he had first walked as a criminal and then later as an angry preacher. In his final days—he had a little less than three months to live—his message became a wholly different one. "Only when mankind would submit to the One God who created all," he told audiences from a place of love for the first time, "only then would mankind even approach the 'peace' of which so much *talk* could be heard . . . but toward which so little *action* was seen."

Malcolm walked away from hatred and toward the light, toward love. He outgrew separatism and embraced the concepts of human rights and human unity.

Each of us, as we fight against injustice, has to be careful. It can so easily harden, coarsen, ruin us. Nietzsche said that those who fight monsters must see to it that they do not become one themselves. It is a testament to Malcolm X's true character that, immersed as he was in evil and hatred, he managed at the end of his life to escape its gravitational pull.

He wasn't perfect. He didn't have time to jettison all his old beliefs (antisemitism, for instance). But the fact that he changed directions that late in the game, after everything he saw and experienced? It gives hope to us lesser humans.

We can't let those sons of bitches turn us into sons of bitches. We can't let inhumanity deprive us of our humanity. We can't let the darkness make us dark—we must always been open to, a conduit for light. Or else the world will become quite dim. *We* will become quite dim.

"Hatred, which could destroy so much," James Baldwin would write, "has never failed to destroy the men who hated, and this [is] an immutable law." Love on the other hand, love protects. It trusts. It hopes. It perseveres. It does not fail.

Love always wins.

Certainly, it is a better way of life.

Is your heart growing or shrinking?

Is your love and compassion and connection for other peo-ple, your hope for a better future, growing or shrinking?

The heart is a muscle. You must make it strong.

Strong, not hard and brittle.

Strong enough to love everything and everyone in all situa-tions.

Strong enough to not break along with the world.

Pay It Forward

~

Ralph Ellison was walking through a building on the grounds of Harvard after dinner one evening when, by chance, he happened to look up. There, in Memorial Hall, which sits on Cambridge Street, just across from Harvard Yard, he saw a long list of names carved into marble.

"I knew its significance almost without knowing," the author later recounted, "and the shock of recognition filled me with a kind of anguish. Something within me cried out 'No!' against that painful knowledge, for I knew that I stood within the presence of Harvard men who had given their young lives to set me free."

Each of these men had given their last full measure of devotion in the American Civil War, sacrificing themselves in the flower of their youth to the idea that *all men are created equal,* liberating Ellison's own grandparents and the country's soul from slavery.

Of course, Ellison had good reason to have thought little of that gesture of humanity, having been born into poverty and racism, experiencing in his early days race riots and lynchings and all the terrible injustices that came from the era of Jim Crow. Besides, he was busy living his own life, fighting his own battles, achieving literary greatness.

So what struck him there so profoundly was an understanding of history that had previously escaped him, a sense of "indebtedness" that would never again leave him.

Nor can it leave us.

All of us bear a great debt to those who sacrificed their yesterdays so that we could have better todays, so that the future would be better.

They crossed oceans. They rotted in prisons. They stepped willingly, shaking with fear, onto great battlefields. They waited. They accepted. They hoped. They endured.

Somebody comforted you when you were brokenhearted. Somebody took care of you when you were small. Somebody worked long hours to support you.

Somebody built these roads. Somebody paid their taxes, somebody invested that money, somebody served in these offices, volunteered after disasters, stood up against wrongdoing. Somebody invented this. Somebody passed these laws, designed these institutions.

Somebody did that for us.

What do we do with this free gift? We must give freely.

Just because no one has asked us to do this, just because our ancestors gave without expecting the third thing . . . there is still a debt. A splendid, spiritual debt attached to existence.

Tammy Duckworth lost both her legs in an instant when her Black Hawk helicopter was shot down by a rocket-propelled grenade. It was her crew that saved her life—her copilot, Chief Warrant Officer 4 Dan Milberg; her door gunner, Kurt Hannemann; her crew chief, Sergeant Chris Fierce—pulling her nearly obliterated body from the wreckage, setting up a defensive perimeter despite their own wounds, and then rushing her to a hospital. It would be days of surgery and years of rehab before she would recover, but she did, eventually working for the Department of Veterans Affairs and later winning a seat in the U.S. Senate.

Yet she remains haunted, not just by the occasional phantom limb pain but also by a certain debt. "I wake up every day," she has explained, "thinking 'I am never going to make [my crew] regret saving my life.'"

We can't just be takers in this life. There was a French king whose philosophy was embodied in the expression *Après moi, le déluge*. After me, the deluge. Or as we say these days, "I'll be gone. You'll be gone." Why care about the consequences?

Um, because someone will get stuck with them? Because somebody cared about the consequences we'd be stuck with?

We must, in light of our indebtedness, not just pay this back but pay it forward.

Because just as we—now living that better life—mattered to someone a long time ago, it should matter to us how future generations live. We have to plant trees for them. We have to start processes, to carry the fire, to light a procession of torches that will continue on after us.

Our job is to make the world a better place to live in, the politician and Stoic LeRoy Percy (the father of Walker Percy's uncle Will) once explained, but only as far as we're able, "always remembering the results will be infinitesimal." Gandhi was not convinced he would live to see the British leave India, and he never promised that *satyagraha* would pay off for the individual. But he believed that each of us was capable of making a small deposit, which, all taken together, could purchase a better future.

We want our children to be able to rest in the shade of the trees we planted, eat the fruit of the trees we planted, breathe the fresh air that those trees filtered. "If my daddy had done this," said one limping, seventy-eight-year-old first-time demonstrator during the civil rights movement, "it would have been a lot better for me." Let's make it so our kids don't have to say that. We should strive to avoid the disappointment of future generations. For that is the ultimate test of any moral society, Dietrich Bonhoeffer wrote, "the kind of world that it leaves to its children."

We don't have to be the leader of some enormous movement to leave the world better. We can help one person. We can be generous, we can be loyal. We can keep our word, we can refuse to give up on somebody. We can be an ally. We can forgive. We can choose a second mountain. We can keep going back, chipping away at a big problem.

There is a poem about an old man on his final journey who comes across a washed-out road. He manages to get to the other side, but when he does, he stops instead of continuing on. There, he labors hard to build a bridge. "Why are you wasting your strength here?" another traveler asked. "You already made it across."

> The builder lifted his old gray head;
> "Good friend, in the path I have come," he said,
> "There followed after me to-day
> A youth whose feet must pass this way.
> This chasm that has been as naught to me
> To that fair-haired youth may a pitfall be;
> He, too, must cross in the twilight dim;
> Good friend, I am building this bridge for him!"

Maybe the bridge won't be finished in our lifetime.

It wasn't for Gandhi. It wasn't for King. Truman could not have known for certain that his reputation would rebound, just as Milk could not have fully predicted just how many would rise in his place.

But this work of a lifetime is also the work that gives life meaning. Having been coated with the stardust of so much goodness, it's our duty—and our *joy*—to sparkle others with it too.

We are coated in the stardust of so much goodness, we can share it with others.

The future depends on it.

Afterword

⌒

I don't think I could have written a book about justice when I was younger. Quite frankly, I'm not sure I would have cared enough.

Like most people, when I was first drawn to Stoicism, I was attracted to what it could do for me. I was looking for stuff I could use. My Stoicism was largely a stern one, about treating the body rigorously, as Seneca said. Getting up early. Running. Fulfilling your potential. Conquering your emotions. Discipline. Fortitude. Grit.

There was a youthful self-centeredness to my early reading of the philosophy—ignore what doesn't concern you, worry primarily about yourself and your own equanimity. If you want to understand how someone ends up being the director of marketing at a publicly traded company shortly after they could legally drink, that's how. It's also how they end up working for some unsavory people and find themselves publishing *Trust Me, I'm Lying: Confessions of a Media Manipulator* at age twenty-five.

Single-mindedness, busy-ness, ambition, and determination—they are quite a cocktail.

But the thing about Stoicism is that it does its work on you. I am lucky that I found Stoicism not just because it kept me calm and collected under pressure, but because as the years went by, the deeper message of the Stoics sunk in. The reason I walked away from marketing instead of becoming an edgelord is because Stoicism had given me the clarity to realize that that was not who I was meant to be. That was not a good direction to take one's life, no matter how rich or powerful it might make you.

You sit with Marcus Aurelius enough and you notice that he refers to "the common good" *a lot* (more than eighty times, as I noted in *The Daily Stoic*). When you look at the actual *lives* of the Stoics (which I did in a book of that title), it's inescapable how strong the theme of justice was in the lives of the lesser-known philosophers who fought against the tyranny and injustices of Nero, Julius Caesar, and other corrupt emperors.

As Stoicism went from ancient Greece to ancient Rome, from lone-wolf philosophers to leaders in civic life, it underwent a transformation. One scholar described this as a "softening," but that's the wrong word. Over the generations, Stoics grew more open, more community-minded, more decent, more generous. They became pillars of society, leaders and heroes whose examples of selflessness and courage and principle have stood for thousands of years.

I can't say the same about myself, but I am definitely a better person now than I was when I started.

I remember once overhearing my father say something about how if you're not a liberal when you're young you have no heart, but if you're not a conservative when you're older, you have no brain. Later I would discover that this was a line popular on talk radio, and actually versions of it date back to the 1870s.

Putting aside our modern political parties, I've come to find this idea to be terribly, terribly sad. Shouldn't it go the exact opposite way? That when you're young you mostly think about yourself and your own needs, but then as you get older, as you experience more, as you meet more and more people, you become more accepting, more open to change, more interested, more willing to help? Yes, it can be hard to maintain idealism in the face of a harsh world, but what kind of life are you living if you become more selfish and colder as you go?

The greatest Stoics, in keeping with their philosophy, went the other way. The emperor Hadrian saw potential in a young Marcus Aurelius, but he would have been stunned at the progress his protégé made, going from an intense young man to a benevolent leader of millions, escaping, as Marcus wrote to himself in *Meditations*, the dreaded scourge of being "Caesarified," being stained purple by his wealth and authority.

This is a journey that we must all go on too, not just avoiding selfishness and cynicism as we age but making sure we are not hardened by our profession or our circumstances. If time and experience don't make you more generous, less threatened by others and their needs, more openhearted, what kind of life is that? Because it sounds more like a prison, like some kind of curse that an enemy would swear on someone in a tragic play, like the cost of selling your soul.

I wouldn't have thought that my books about an obscure school of ancient philosophy would put me in the manufacturing business, but Daily Stoic has grown into a publishing company, a media company, an e-commerce operation, and a bookstore in a small town in Texas. It's a small business in the sense that there are only six or seven of us in the office every day—and yet it's not really small at all, given its revenues and its reach, which now extends to tens of millions of people every month.

The reason most companies outsource and subcontract isn't just because it's cheaper. It's because out of sight means out of mind. It means not having to think about the realities of what your business does and is, who it affects.

So as I've built out my business, I've tried to ask myself the questions that the Stoics were struggling with even back in the days of Antipater—the ones about transparency, about externalization, about downstream consequences.

At Daily Stoic, we sell challenge coins inspired by philosophical concepts (one says *Memento Mori,* another *Amor Fati*), which many readers find central to their daily practice of Stoicism. After receiving many bids, I learned that it would be significantly cheaper to manufacture those coins in China than in the United States. I've read about the Uighurs in concentration camps there, I know about the labor conditions overseas, I know that it's not great for the environment to needlessly ship stuff across the Pacific.

But ethics come attached to business expenses: It was out of my wallet that the higher cost per unit would come. I would be the one who would have to go to customers and ask them to pay a higher price. It was me who was vulnerable to knockoffs and imitators.

Ultimately, I made the decision to work with a great American company, Wendell's, which has been in business in Minnesota since 1882. It wasn't cheaper but it was cleaner and still more than profitable. We're both succeeding as we pursue our own interests, making Adam Smith proud. But it's worth remembering that before his work on capitalism, Adam Smith studied Stoicism and wrote in his book *A Theory of Moral Sentiments* about operating as though there is an impartial spectator on your shoulder, watching and judging the decisions that you make.

No one throws you a parade when you do the right thing. Karma, as much as we'd like for it to be true, has a funny way of not coming around. One of my stranger hobbies is picking up trash. I have a bag, one of those sticks with a spike on it, and I go up and down the country roads where we live. I have disposed of dumpsters worth of garbage over the years (including, most disturbingly, the carcasses of poached animals and dogs dumped from dogfighting rings). The police don't seem to care and neither do most of my neighbors. Karma? It doesn't matter how many nails I get off the ground, it hasn't stopped me from getting flats.

But we don't do it for the recognition. We do it because if we don't, who will?

We start small and we build. I found out that Wendell's was individually shrink-wrapping each of our coins. They explained the protective benefits of the plastic—and that it was cheap—and I'm sure 95 percent of the world's excessive packaging exists for those reasons. But with a single decision, I had more impact than a lifetime of litter cleanup.

After Putin's tanks rolled into Ukraine with the support of Belarus's president, Alexander Lukashenko, I had to take a hard look at the business I was doing with a bespoke producer of leather-bound editions of several books I put out. Ultimately, it was not illegal to work in Belarus and it cost me twice as much to find a British supplier who could do what Belarus had been doing, but as they say, it's not a principle until it costs you money.

Could I have done it if it was a multimillion-dollar decision? I have no idea. I have sympathy for CEOs who face those choices. But I've gotten better at making expensive decisions: Deciding not to sell stuff I thought was lame and wouldn't use (even if customers asked for it). Deciding not to accept advertisers who sell alcohol or weed or promote gambling. Deciding not to contribute to the grossness of Black Friday and Cyber Monday (the two most lucrative sales days of the year) and to use those slots for annual food drives instead ($627,000 raised so far, roughly 6.2 million meals).

We make the little decisions so we can make the big ones, even if no one is looking, even if nobody cares but us.

One thing that has come to serve as a north star for me— given that I didn't invent Stoicism and lay no claim to it other than the fact that people seem to like what I have to say—is written on a notecard next to my desk: "Are you being a good steward of Stoicism?"

Having access to the unsubscribe stats for the Daily Stoic email, I can see clearly that at even the slightest mention about our obligations to each other, about issues like racism or inequality, I will lose readers and customers. *What would Seneca say about you using Stoicism to talk about politics?* angry people will write in . . . forgetting that not only did Seneca serve in government but that he said Stoicism *obligated* a philosopher to participate in political life (in fact, many of the Stoics were literally politicians). It's a test we face in a world driven by algorithms— do we tell people what they want to hear? Or do we say and do what we think needs to be done?

Stoicism is particularly attractive to young men who are struggling for purpose and direction in life. I know this because I once was one of them. I had issues with my father. I belonged to no tribe, I had no war to prove myself in, no band of brothers to support me. Every generation feels like their role in society is precarious, but for a generation young people have faced recessions and terrorism and political unrest and failing institutions, repeated shocks that have quite tested their faith in the future.

We have a generation of lost young men. Women are thriving in school, in higher education, and in the workplace in encouraging and inspiring ways. Men in America and in many other countries, the statistics show, seem to be in a kind of doom loop. They're struggling. They're angry. They're angry that on top of their own struggles, they're supposed to care about other people who are struggling for different reasons. That they have to consider other people's disadvantages, other injustices than the ones they're dealing with.

It shouldn't surprise us that demagogues and grifters would step into this void, playing off these insecurities, offering (mis) guidance as well as grievances. They've taken the tenets of Stoic philosophy, perverted it, mixed it with equal parts toxic masculinity and ressentiment—absorbing right-wing talking points and normalizing a kind of modern-day Know-Nothingism. This is clearly good business, as some of the massive online audiences of certain controversial figures indicate. They are speaking to people who were ignored and feel mistreated, and perhaps it was inevitable that someone would step in to meet this demand.

All I know is that *I won't be one of those people*. With every unsubscribe and accusation that I've gone "woke," my determination to counterprogram grows.

There has not been much karma in it. The last few years have been marked for my family and me by almost constant harassment from trolls and extremists for stands we've taken against book banning, for our support of gay and trans rights, for women's rights, for volunteering at vaccine clinics, and for working to remove Confederate monuments from our town.

But I have two boys of my own, and I am made responsible. I feel compelled to demonstrate a different path. I carry a debt that I must pay by being a good father and a good citizen.

It's not virtue signaling to push back against cruelty and indifference. It doesn't make you a "social justice warrior" to speak out for kindness and fairness and inalienable rights. But even if it was, is anything *better* to be a warrior for than justice and or anything better to signal than virtue? What has to happen to your brain to be *opposed* to those things?

During the pandemic, one journalist noted a trend he called "COVID stoicism," this attitude of *I'm not scared of this virus. I don't need to wear a mask or get a vaccine like some pussy. Why should I have to change one iota of my behavior for other people?* It's a kind of reactionary, almost performative indifference, an inability to conceive of "how the other half lives," that not everyone is young or healthy or has the same access to medical care. Fundamentally, a public health crisis obliterates the fiction of separateness—the lie of individualism. The pandemic should have reminded us how we are all in this together, how we are only as safe as the most vulnerable among us.

Over one *million* Americans died. Globally, millions more perished. Many of them did not have to. If we had all made better decisions more of them would be alive today.

This is the opposite of Stoicism. We're not here for ourselves. We can't watch the world burn. Our job is to try to save the world . . . and failing that, at least we can try to not be part of the problem.

My study of history has led me to believe that there is a kind of dark matter inside the human race. It's different from evil—which, of course, everyone is capable of—but it is a kind of dark oppositional energy that goes from issue to issue, era to era. It's rooted in self-interest, self-preservation, in fear, in not wanting to be inconvenienced, not wanting to change, not wanting to have to get involved. It manifests itself a thousand ways, but once you know how to recognize it, you spot it everywhere.

It was there in big moments in history. The prosecution of Socrates, the judicial cruelty of Pontius Pilate, the Inquisition, the Confederacy, the exploitation of colonialism, the thwarting of Reconstruction, collaboration in Vichy France, the people who shouted slurs and jeers at Ruby Bridges as she walked into school for the first time. It's there in the little and modern moments too, the exhausting obstruction of your NIMBY neighbor at a city council meeting, the bullying of librarians for doing their jobs, shrugging off another mass shooting and the acceleration of climate change because the solution is politically difficult, the Thin Blue Line flag, the excesses of cancel culture, the disowning of a child who has just come out as gay or trans, proposing that we just "let 'er rip" when a virus is ravaging and killing.

This dark energy is within each of us, but we also have better angels of our nature. Which will win out?

I particularly liked Marcus Aurelius's observation, written during his own devastating pandemic, that there are two types of plagues. One can take your life, he said, but the one to worry about is the one that can destroy your character. One of the most indelible images we have of Marcus is the man breaking down and weeping over the countless victims who had been lost to the virus of his time . . . and no doubt also venting his frustration at the cruelty and indifference by people he thought he knew, at how much harder it turned out to be to try to do the right thing.

Any philosophy that hardens you to the plight of other people, any philosophy that punches down (at people who are different, at people who have less) instead of up (as the Stoic Opposition did to Caesar and Nero and Domitian), any philosophy that rages instead of loves?

These ideas are the plague of our time.

If there is one thing I didn't get to cover enough in this book, it was the topic of love and relationships. I've always felt that the Stoics didn't go far enough in connecting friendship and affection to the virtue of justice. There was a story I wanted to include about Charles de Gaulle in *Courage Is Calling* and again in this book that I couldn't find the right place for: In 1928, he and his wife had a child named Anne. She had Down syndrome—although in the parlance of the day, people would have referred to her by far less kind terms and most families, tragically, shipped such children off to institutions. Of all that de Gaulle accomplished, of all that he did for France and the world, I found his relationship with his daughter to be one of the most impressive.

"She did not ask to come into the world," he said. "We shall do everything to make her happy." But it was not just what he did for her, in the end, but what she did for him. She softened him, opened him up, made him a better person. "I believe she played a profound part in his life," a close friend would say. "In London, it was when he walked holding her hand that he used to reflect, and perhaps the tone of his reflections would have been somehow different had they not been born in the presence of pain."

In the afterword of *Discipline Is Destiny,* I talked about hitting a wall and nearly needing to ask my publisher for an extension. It was actually on this book that I did take that step . . . for very different reasons. I decided to push the completion of this book back a year so that I could be a better dad and husband and boss and human being.

All artists are profoundly selfish on some level, their commitment to their craft naturally consuming them, subsuming everything else underneath it. Wright Thompson—the sportswriter whose pieces on Michael Jordan, Tiger Woods, Muhammad Ali, and Ted Williams I have used in many of my books—talked about *the cost of these dreams.* It takes a lot out of a person to be great at what they do, but it takes a lot out of the people around them too. Their spouse, their children, their staff, the people they compete against, the strangers they bump into on the street. The cost of success is paid largely not by us but by those who love us, who support us, who work tirelessly for us (who, even if well paid, are likely to not get the credit they deserve).

But ultimately, it doesn't matter what kind of work you do or what you accomplish. In the end, you're measured by how you treat the people closest to you. This extension was a gift. It was also a challenge. It dredged up stuff that a much busier, less reachable version of myself just didn't have to deal with.

I got a better sense of the load others had been carrying for me, the sacrifices they made for me—so I could follow my dreams. I can't fully imagine what it's like to live with me on a day-to-day basis, let alone be married to me all these years, but I've come to understand that it was not exactly easy on my wife, for one. It's been an uncomfortable process trying to make amends for that, but if we can't stare at our own past, our own mistakes in the face, we'll just go on continuing to make them.

As I reengaged with the material and started writing again, I've had to practice a different kind of discipline in my work, focusing more on balance and more on putting other people and their needs first. But the unexpected benefit was that after making the somewhat scary decision to put the professional behind the personal, I think the final product actually did turn out to be better.

Plus, I am happier and my house is a more equitable one.

I've tried to take that energy back out into the world.

I found out a while back that one of my favorite employees had been self-dealing, creating a company that they then awarded inflated contracts to, pocketing tens of thousands of dollars from the work they subcontracted.

I was so angry. So angry.

This was a crossroads moment for them, but also for me. A younger me would not only have wanted blood but gotten it, needing to prove I was not a person to mess with. Instead, I tried to look at it in "the calm light of mild philosophy," tried to practice this grace I was writing about.

In *Les Misérables,* Bishop Myriel lets the thief keep the stolen goods—*use this to become an honest man.* That seemed like a bridge too far. Instead we worked out an arrangement where any illicit gains were disgorged. Surprisingly, they wanted to keep their job, and there was a weaker part of me that just wanted to pretend it didn't happen. But how would that be fair to everyone else in the company? ("Justice is an awful tyrant," Truman said.) Still, I could let them keep their dignity and their future. They could learn from this and grow ... wherever they end up.

Will I come to regret this? Maybe. Maybe their character is already formed and it's too late. But I feel good knowing that mine is still intact, that my own capacity for empathy has been enlarged in the process. Forgiveness, they say, is a gift you give yourself. My aim was to spare myself bitterness, paranoia, resentment, distraction, and guilt. My aim was to not do anything that I would come to regret and to not throw time and energy and money into getting "justice" dressed up as revenge or punishment.

For all the problems that problematic people cause us, the Stoics want us to remember, they present us with an equal amount of opportunity. It wasn't a fun experience but it did shape the writing of this book.

My children, perhaps like yours, are not particularly interested in my work. In fact, as I wrote this afterword, my oldest son picked up a copy of *The Daily Stoic* and said, "Oh, that's Daddy's book, *The Daily Butthole*."

It's always good to be humbled . . .

Although I suspect this book won't be the bestselling of the virtue series, if there was one book I'd like my children to someday read, it would be this one—as I have written it for them as a kind of ethical will.

I said before, what attracted me at first to Stoicism was what it could do for me. Through the years and my own struggles, I'm more convinced than ever that to choose this philosophy means accepting a certain responsibility. It means assuming a certain stewardship.

It's one even the best of us will struggle to live up to.

But we are better for the trying.

It will challenge and shame and overwhelm us.

But it will be the most meaningful and rewarding thing we ever do.

At the end of our lives, we won't care that much if people think we were hardworking or that the risks we've taken in our careers have paid off. We'll want someone to say, "That was a good person. They were honest and decent and generous and loyal and kind. They made the world a better place."

Life is short.

Be good. Do good.

Love and be loved.

Try to leave the place better than you found it.

Do the right thing.

Right now.

Ryan Holiday
Miramar Beach, FL
2023

What To Read Next?

Now For most people, bibliographies are boring. For those who love to read, it's the best part. In the case of this book, which relied on so many wonderful authors and thinkers, I could not possibly fit the entire bibliography in the book. Instead, I've prepared a full list not only of all the great books that influenced the ideas you've just read, but also what I got out of them and why you might like to read them. To get this list, please just email books@therightthingrightnow.com or go to therightthingrightnow.com/books.

CAN I GET EVEN MORE BOOK RECOMMENDATIONS?

YES. You can also sign up for my list of monthly book recommendations (now in its second decade). The list has grown to include more than two hundred thousand people all over the world and recommended thousands of life-changing books. RyanHoliday.net/readingnewsletter. I'll start you off with ten awesome books, I know you'll love.

Acknowledgments

The other chapter I hoped to squeeze into this book but struggled to find a place for was one on gratitude. None of us would be here without the help of so many people, and certainly this book would not exist without countless friends and acts of service. I am grateful for my publisher, Portfolio, and the folks there who published not just my first book but all of them since. I owe much to my agent, Stephen Hanselman, for his support and advocacy. Specifically, this book was better for the notes from Dolores Molina (my bonus grandmother), David Roll, Sam Koppelman, Peter Singer, Nils Parker, Dear Beloved, Tyler Shultz, Hristo Vassilev, and Billy Oppenheimer. Thank you to the late Paul Woodruff for the encouragement and most of all for how you modeled the philosopher's life, even up to the very end. The entire Daily Stoic universe could not function without the tireless work of people like Dawson Carroll, Deezie Brown, Chelsea Dobrot, Rachel Penberg, Jess Davidson, Brent Underwood, and many others. I am grateful and indebted to the many authors, thinkers, and heroic figures whose writing, ideas, and lives filled out the pages of this book—and indeed all my work. I could not do it without you . . . I can only try to pay things forward. And as I said in the afterword, I owe the most to my family. Samantha, thank you for all your patience and understanding and love. To my boys, Clark and Jones, thank you for giving me something to look forward to waking up to and coming home to. Jones, you asked that I mention bunnies in this book, so consider that done. Bunny, bunny, bunny.

Learn more with Ryan Holiday

Join the millions of readers around the world who turn to Ryan Holiday's books for their blend of ancient wisdom and modern expertise: covering culture and the human condition, these books offer tools for success and fulfilment in the busy everyday.

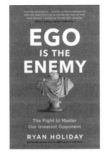
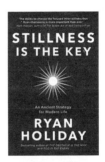

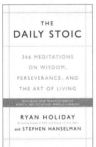
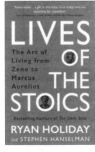
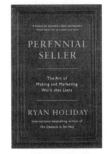

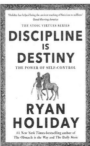
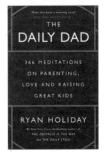

Interested in learning
even more about Stoicism?

Visit

DailyStoic.com/email

to sign up for a daily email,

engage in discussion, get advice,

and more.